MESSAGES BEHIND SHAPES

MUSIC, BIOGEOMETRY, LIGHT, WATER, WORD

BY MILENA

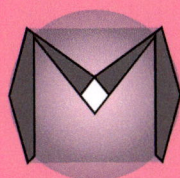

M PUBLISHING

CONTENTS

ONE IS MANY
– SHAPE ARCHETYPES

There are many ways to interpret the *Genesis* story featured in the sacred books of Jews, Muslims and Christians. The one that follows is focused on the geometry of the primal Creation. It bears a resemblance to the view that **Drunvalo Melchizedek** presents in his book *The ANCIENT SECRET of the FLOWER OF LIFE*[1-1].

The primary Creation was the moment when the first sphere appeared. It was a creative expression of the mysterious Power that manifested itself within the primordial Void. It is the One we will symbolise by a circle throughout this chapter.

To further the exploration of the self, One needed to provide an opportunity to relate to "something". Thus, through self-mirroring on the *first day* of *Genesis* the *vesica pisces* was formed, and the essential desire of Creation for growth and newness established a pattern for continuous transformation.

Vesica pisces (Fig. 1.2) is the data of archetypal proportions of regular shapes on which the entirety of Creation is based. Nature clothes these shapes in different garments, delivering an amazing variety of appearances.

God has created us in order that we may become partakers of the divine nature, in order that we might enter into eternity, and that we might appear alike unto Him, being deified by that grace out of which all things that exist have come.

St. Maximus the Confessor[1-2]

▶ *1.1 – The first Creation: the Primordial Void expresses itself as One (sphere)*

In the linear, polarity initiates movement. When one is in substance, the answers are provided continually and questions aren't needed.

Flo Aeveia Magdalena[1-3]
(Sunlight on the Water)

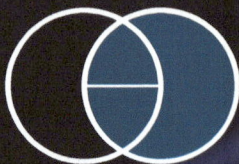

There is only one relationship: you with you. When you get that one right, you can attract all the other relationships you choose.

The Group through Steve Rother[1-4]

I have already told you how Creation began, when thought came forth and worked upon the ocean of Love that I am. It was My desire to share Love. It was My need to give Love that created the explosion that was the idea of Creation. The moment that thought touched the Love a great reaction ensued, and every increment of thought that I had, every image that flashed through Me of billions of ways to give My Love, became clothed in Love. In the great moment and by the energy that is thought, all of Creation came to be.

One great union of thought and Love and Everything That Is came forth. Oh, it was indeed a 'Big Bang', dear ones! It was smoke and fire and great whirling winds and billions of golden lights shooting forth in flight, taking on their form as the substance of Love wrapped around them. The further something flew from Me, the 'cooler' the Love that clothed it became and, thus, the more dense or more physical.

The Messages from God through Yael and Doug Powell[1-6]

▲ *1.2 – The first day of Creation – vesica pisces*

When there is one, there is no distance, but where there is distance, there is length. Of length is longing born. – **Daniel Winter**[1-5]

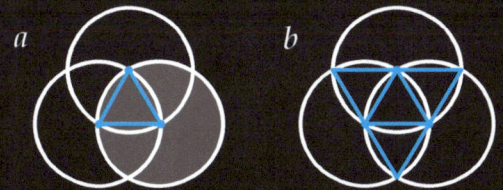

1.3 – When a story of a sphere becomes a story of a triangle – the second day of Creation manifests the triangle and the 2nd dimension.

The first triangle (Fig. 1.3a) appears within a fractal pattern of self-iteration (Fig. 1.3b) which we find in the so-called Sierpinski triangle. Thus the appearance of the first triangle means the appearance of a potentially endless number of triangles.

T h e word *day* in the context of *Genesis* carries the concept of an era, epoch, or a stage of development. As we have seen in figure 1.2, prompted by the urge to express itself, on the *first day* the first sphere created the *vesica pisces*. The shifting of the centre of the first sphere described a line. Hence, the so called *first dimension* was born as a line within the *vesica pisces*.

On the *second day*, the three spheres defined a surface by the three lines bounding their centres in an equilateral triangle and the so-called *second dimension* was manifested. The triangle is the first form that emerged from the absolute Void and through the mouth of the *vesica pisces*, hence it can be seen as the cardinal surface unit in the matrix of Creation (Fig. 1.3). Once it appeared on the life stage, the triangle continued to live in all subsequent shapes providing structural stability throughout Creation.

If we illustrate the process of Creation as an outer expansion, then the emerging spheres do not overlap but merely touch one another (Fig. 1.4). The appearance of the four spheres simultaneously touching each other, provided a template for the first volume – a tetrahedron. Thus, in this context, the *third day* of Creation manifested the *third dimension*. Interestingly, this case, when the biggest number of spheres can maintain mutual contact, is also a symbol of the geometry of our first four cells from the moment we are conceived.

The absolute reality will have every colour, sound, etc. and its opposite. This means everything put together without selection, making a total energy soup, if perceived in its totality would produce nothing. A nothing that includes everything, just like putting all colours of the spectrum together, would give the full light which is colourless. Similarly, all sounds together would cancel each other. Thus absolute reality is everything and nothing.

Dr Ibrahim F. Karim[1-7]

The days that followed, according to the calendar of the primeval Creation, provided more information necessary for the appearance of further forms. Pertaining to the evolvement through the *vesica pisces*, new spherical emanations of the same radius appearing around the central one in an already established pattern, will eventually complete a figure that illustrates the relation between Six and One within an orderly unity of Seven. It is a geometrical symbol of the first six days of *Genesis*, considered to be its *first pattern* (Fig. 1.4, 1.6).

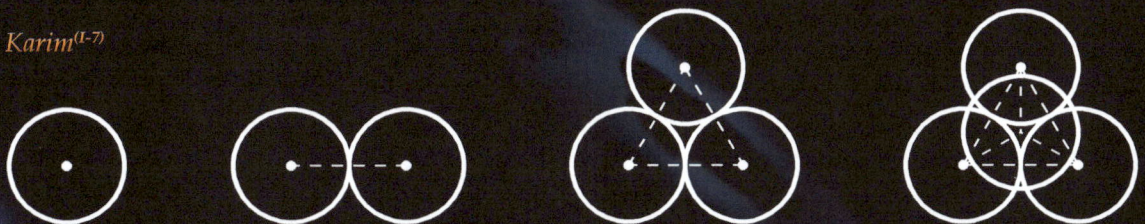

1.4 – The unfolding of the 1st, 2nd and 3rd dimensions through outer expansion

1.5 – Shapes born from the first pattern of Genesis: 1 - tetrahedron, 2 - cube, 3 - octahedron and 4 - icosahedron. The shape (6) is composed of three identical golden rectangles. It is the skeleton common to all the Platonic solids. 5 - star-tetrahedron.

1

2

3

5

5

6

1.6 – The first pattern of Genesis – Creation after six days and the torus on it

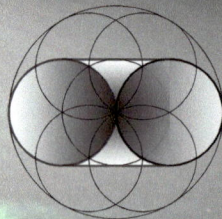

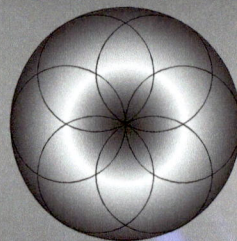

For in six days the Lord made the heavens and the earth, the sea, and all that is in them, but he rested on the seventh day...

The Bible (Exodus 20:11)

GOD is the One who created the heavens and the earth, and everything between them in six days, then assumed all authority...

The Quran (32:4)

The Genesis story of old states that the heavens and Earth were created in six days and on the seventh day, God rested. A cosmic or universal day contains trillions and trillions of your earthly days and, indeed, it has taken an incomprehensible amount of time to create this universe. We have explained that after the Supreme Creator stirred and radiated forth an inexplicable number of fragments of ITSELF and initiated the creation of the Omniverse, IT went into repose as an Omnipotent Observer.

Archangel Michael through Ronna Herman[1-8]

In the beginning there were six – say holy books indicating the significance of the number Six for the primal completion. The next Creational steps are hugely influenced by this stage and further self-exploration of the One continues endlessly, both inwards and outwards. We also experience these two paths. One path is an expansion of our domain perceivable from outside and prompted by our desire for more friends, diplomas and gadgets, while the other is our selfward journey as the spiritual expansion aimed at acquiring the highest human virtues.

1.7 – If the universe is made of waves, according to Daniel Winter, its primal shape is the sine wave. There is a connection between sine waves (a) and the torus shape (b).

a

b

ONE IS MANY

Two ways to store memory in a compressible medium:
A – spin vector thruster and B – charge vector thruster.
If the geometry is optimized, the result in both cases
is the same and the physics of the mechanical world
merges back into its primary cause.
This dual aspect of the toroid, the coupled spin geometry and the surface thrust
geometry, makes it function as the archetypal shape and operative principle of going
in and out of mechanical creation, which is the true physics of life force and individual
perception.

Frank van den Bovenkamp[1-9]
(Heart Coherence team)

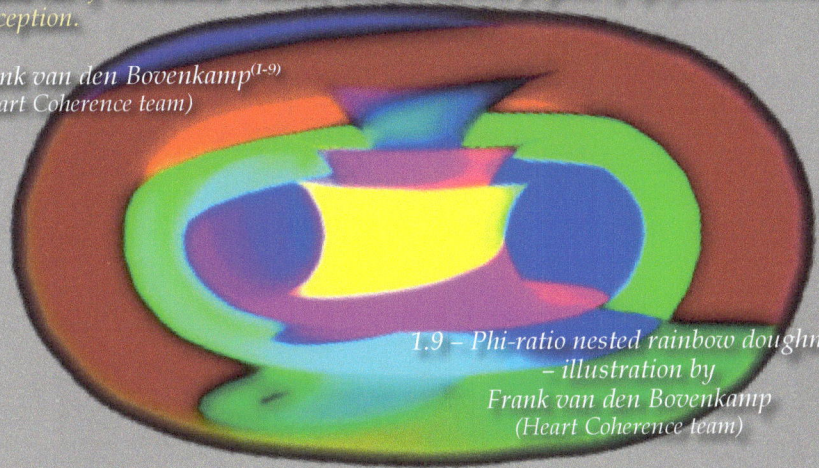

1.8 – The secret of torus
– illustration by
Frank van den Bovenkamp

1.9 – Phi-ratio nested rainbow doughnut
– illustration by
Frank van den Bovenkamp
(Heart Coherence team)

REACHING THE INFINITY

In the first geometrical pattern of *Genesis* (Fig. 1.5, 1.6), every pair of opposite circles, taken without the central circle, can serve as a starting point for illustrating the endless inward capacity of the Primordial Power (Fig.1.11). The same drawing is also a metaphor for the richness of our personal inner potential which we gradually activate while seeking out our godly self.

It is not difficult to envisage the same process directed outwardly by tangentially adding one circle, identical to the biggest existing one, and surrounding them both by a new double-radius circle in comparison to the added one (Fig. 1.10). Continuing this process will create a chain of endlessly augmenting circles. Figures 1.10 and 1.11 illustrate the fact that our perception depends on our choice of focus, and its boundaries. With the change of boundaries, in a new context, tiny becomes vast and vast becomes tiny. Infinity dwells in each particle of Creation.

The shift in your reality is happening on many levels simultaneously. A reality is both a physical and a spiritual construct. The Creator forged physicality out of a number of limitless possibilities. Each range of possibilities was embodied in a specific Creation, and each Creation led explicably to the next. All ten Creations together forged the unlimited whole put forth by the Creator at the moment of their mutual creation. What you see around you is merely an iota of what actually exists. Yet, when you go into the spiritual realms, the wholeness of this divine thought quickly becomes apparent. Behind all this is a grand sacred plan which is now revealing itself to you. Your current purpose, therefore, is to go beyond your limited physical self and discover how this amazing blueprint is to be realized. As you do this, you become wondrously aware of the divine magic behind its construction. As your awareness of this and of your ultimate connection to every other Being in this reality grows, you become increasingly unwilling to believe in the dogma of the concepts that supposedly govern this reality.

Galactic Federation of Light
through Sheldan Nidle[1-10]

▼ *1.10 –*
Limitless
outward
expansion/
multiplication
is a reflection
of inner potential

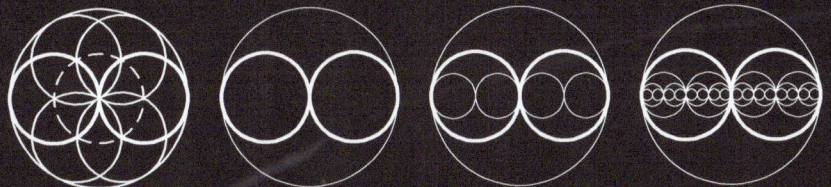

▲ *1.11 – This division/multiplication, which is also the*
graph of a sine wave or a light wave, is based on a binary
sequence: 2, 4, 8, 16, 32, 64…
and continues forever inwardly

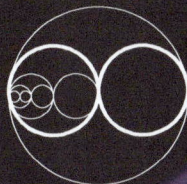

The Chinese symbol known as the *Yin-Yang* depicts the dual nature of Creation. *Yin* and *Yang* are its prime principles, like two charges. Through their dynamic relationship, all forms and states of Total emerge.

Yin represents the weak, dark, cold, contracting, and passive forces of existence while *Yang* is its exact opposite being strong, light, hot, expanding and active. These two aspects of One, however antagonistic, are complementary at the same time.

▲ *1.12 – It takes two to complete the binary sequence:
up and down
(left and right – on and off
– in and out – concave and convex…)
Life is an experience of joint opposites dancing together.*

*The Way is perfect like vast space
where nothing is lacking
and nothing is in excess.*

*Indeed, it is due to our choosing to accept
or reject that we do not see
the true nature of things.*

*Live neither in the entanglements of outer things,
nor in inner feelings of emptiness.*

*Be serene in the oneness of things
and such erroneous
views will disappear by themselves.*

*When you try to stop activity to achieve passivity
your very effort fills you with activity.*

*As long as you remain in one extreme
or the other you will never know Oneness.*

Seng Ts'an[(1-11)]

▼ *1.13 – Yin-Yang depicts the prime divine principles*

*Everything has both
yin and yang in it
and from their rise-and-fall
coupling comes new life.*

*Lao Tzu[(1-12)]
(Tao Te Ching)*

*I am the wave.
I am the creative movement.
I am the system through which
the substance is always infused.
I am participating in the viable,
creative means through which
this universe is emerging.*

*Flo Aeveia Magdalena
(Sunlight on the Water)*

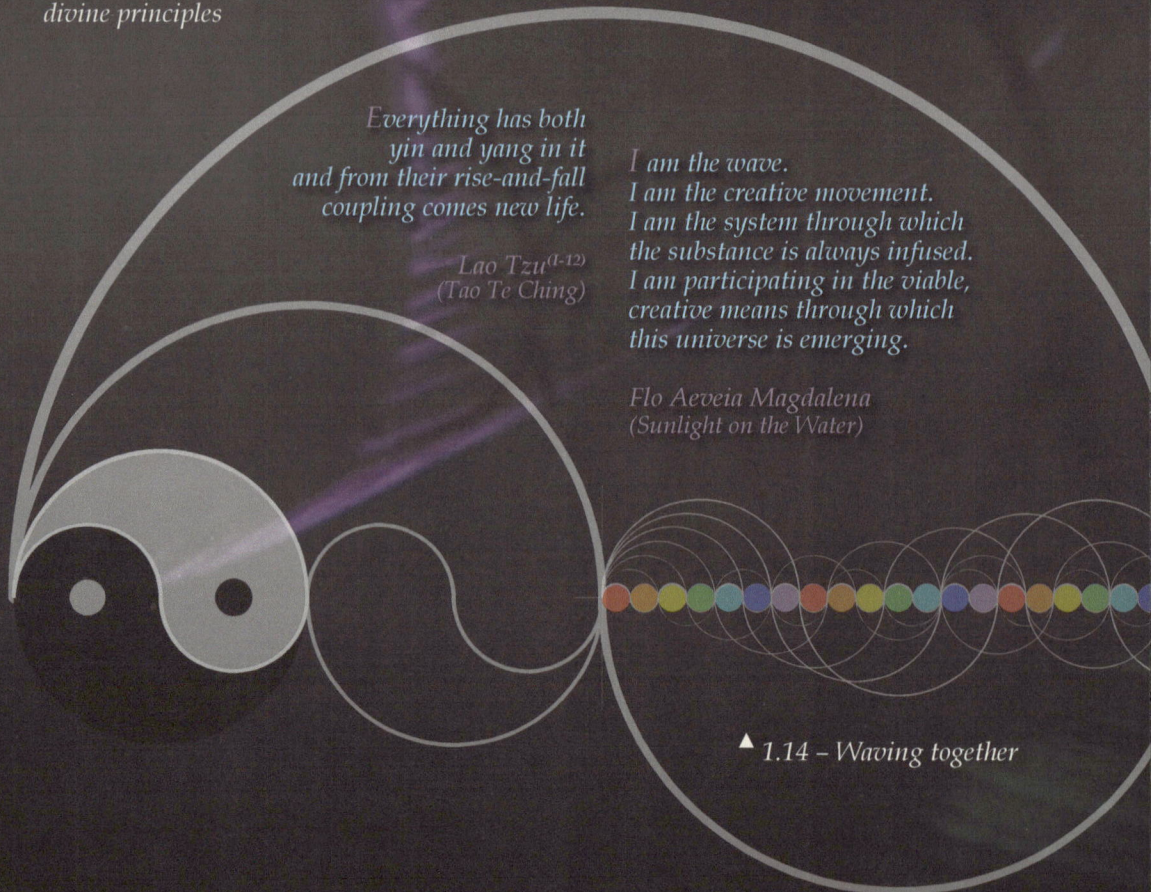

▲ *1.14 – Waving together*

The way *Yin* and *Yang* are inscribed in the circle, in One, suggests their continuous movement and transformation, as well as the notion that everything holds the seed of its opposite.

Within the blackness of the *Yin* there is a white spot of *Yang* and within the whiteness of the *Yang* a black spot of *Yin*, to remind us how nothing is solely black or white but a fertile field where seeds of the opposite value provide potential for change. In an eternal flow, opposites destroy and re-create themselves while constantly maintaining a mutual balance within the whole they make. The *Yin-Yang* is a perfect graphical symbol of the principles of eternal transformation and divine equilibrium.

ONE IS MANY

ETERNAL BECOMING

From the first pattern of *Genesis* (Fig. 1.6), Creation continues towards infinity following the principle established with the appearance of the *vesica pisces*.

Processes, inward and outward, are happening simultaneously and can be observed as a rhythm of being. A universe also goes through periods of expansion and contraction while following the programmes of its own essence. Each new experience redefines the entire Creation and so, against the background of infinity, Creation continues to learn about itself. This phenomenon we would call *LIFE*.

So God is always busy arting throughout His own Creation. He is visionary, bold, playful, and dares to periodically start all over again, from the beginning, recycling the elements of the game. Rejuvenating His own Self through eternal *Becoming*, God's **IS**ness thus canonises the *change* into His first existential principle.

FLOWER OF LIFE

Each new day of Creation manifested one new sphere. These new spheres interlocked with the six spheres which were formed during the first six days (Fig. 1.6). At that moment, the entire Creation comprised thirteen spheres that illustrate the relationship between the numbers One, Six, Seven (1+6=7) and Thirteen (7+6=13) (Fig. 1.15). Following the established geometrical pattern of interweaving, yet another generation of six spheres appeared and created the figure made of 19 spheres (Fig. 1.16a, 1.16b). This level of Creation is the birth point of the *flower of life,* fully defined only when the 36 spheres, from the next two generations of spheres, lend their appropriate segments to it (1.16c).

▲ 1.16 – (a, b) The third pattern of Genesis composed of 13 white + 6 red = 19 whole spheres;
(c) The flower of life figure completed by the adding of spherical segments (orange), borrowed from the 36 spheres of the next succession

▲ 1.15 – (a) The second pattern of Genesis made of 13 spheres (7+6);
(b) The same pattern shown with 42 equal triangles (7x6)

1.17 – The flower of life based on 19 overlapping identical spheres (a) and, within it, the perfect seal figure composed of 7 perfectly touching identical spheres/circles (b)

Your God is One God; there is no god but He, Most Gracious, Most Merciful. – The Quran (2:163)

The resulting figure is often shown surrounded by two concentric spheres, although they are not its essential structural part (Fig. 1.17). Nineteen whole spheres and the parts of 36 spheres make all together 55 spheres involved in the making of the *flower of life*. Here we find the *master number* 55 behind a pattern of the highest order, symmetry and creative potential.

The *flower of life* is a geometrical collection of archetypal proportions and as such holds many secrets of Creation. It has been recorded in the artwork of the world's ancient cultures such as China, India, Turkey, Israel and Greece. The oldest example of the *flower of life* was found in the Temple of **Osiris**, at Abydos in Egypt.

With its vocabulary, the *flower of life* illustrates the symmetry of Creation and an orderly interconnectedness of all the elements within it. Somewhere in the geometry of this infinite flower, each one of us resides sharing the charge and potential of the whole. We are the petals touching one another and complementing one another in the perfection and beauty of this divine structure.

From the *flower of life*, which is based on nineteen whole spheres, we could now glance at *The Quran*. The number 19 is its consistent structural determinant, as **Dr Rashad Khalifa** discovered in 1974[I-14]. For example, this holy book has 114 chapters (19x6) and the opening verse 1:1, *Bismillahir-Rahmanir-Rahim (In the name of God, Most Gracious, Most Merciful)*, is composed of nineteen Arabic letters.

The Greeks and the Romans had a grip on Sacred Geometry and their empires were founded on this knowledge. Everything is basically built on the 'phi' ratio of the Fibonacci sequence and within the Flower of Life. Anything that is not built within the ratios that are to be found in the Flower of Life will not be able to be fully energised by Spirit. For those of you in this room this night who are engineers or architects or those of you who are doing some type of building or creative work – you will do well to study the Flower of Life and to understand how Sacred Geometry works and how it is created. The entire Universe can be found in the Flower of Life and if you truly wish your creations to work – then your creations should also be founded in Sacred Geometry.

Kryon through David Brown[I-15]

Anything not supporting a positive flow of love and life will gently flow away and crumble to dust. So it is important that the architects of the planet fully understand Sacred Geometry and the rules of the Flower of Life. The Flower of Life is in all your hearts, so close your eyes and go into your heart and see for yourself this Flower of Life; and if you cannot see it then allow the energy of this flower to gently expand throughout your heart and allow it to awaken you to the truth of sacred geometry and to the truth of life on earth, for this Flower of Life is where truth begins and where life begins. It has within it all secrets of creation and part of being a human is being a creator; you create your own life and your own destiny and the more you clear your emotional centres and the emotional fields, the more you step into love and the more you make love through your heart, the more beautiful your creations become, the more beautiful life becomes and the easier the energy flows through your hear, the stronger and more profound is your connection to Spirit.

Kryon
through David Brown

Furthermore, there are 19 verses where the word *Wahid* (meaning *One* in Arabic) is used to refer to, or to characterise, *Allah* as ONE. The interesting detail is that the alphanumerical value of the word *One (Wahid)* in the Arabic language is also nineteen[I-16].

The ways the number 19 appears throughout *The Quran* are many and it makes sense to wonder about the real reason behind it. Is it just an illustration of our sacred books being written by an electronic system, or more than that[I-17]? We will know the truth when we are ready for it.

Concealed in the geometry of the *flower of life* are two important figures: the *seed of life* and the *tree of life* (Fig. 1.19).

b

a

◄ ▲ 1.18
– *Within every flower of life, based on 19 whole spheres, a cube-octahedron can be found (a). A cube-octahedron engages 13 closely packed spheres of the same radius, while the centres of 12 of those spheres determine its vertices. All edges and all distances from the vertices to the centre of this quasiregular polyhedron are of equal length (b). No other geometric form exhibits such a property. Due to this vector equilibrium, cube-octahedron is seen as a system of an exact energetic balance of (reversible) implosion and explosion tendencies. It is a model of stillness – a zero-state, which all forms and events emerge from.*

SEED OF LIFE

The *seed of life* itself holds the information of a *tree*. This *tree
of life* is defined by ten connected dots or spheres.

▼ 1.19 – *The seed of life figure (a) and
the tree of life figure (b) that emerges
from this seed*

▼ 1.20 – *The flower
of life conceals the
12-point tree of life*

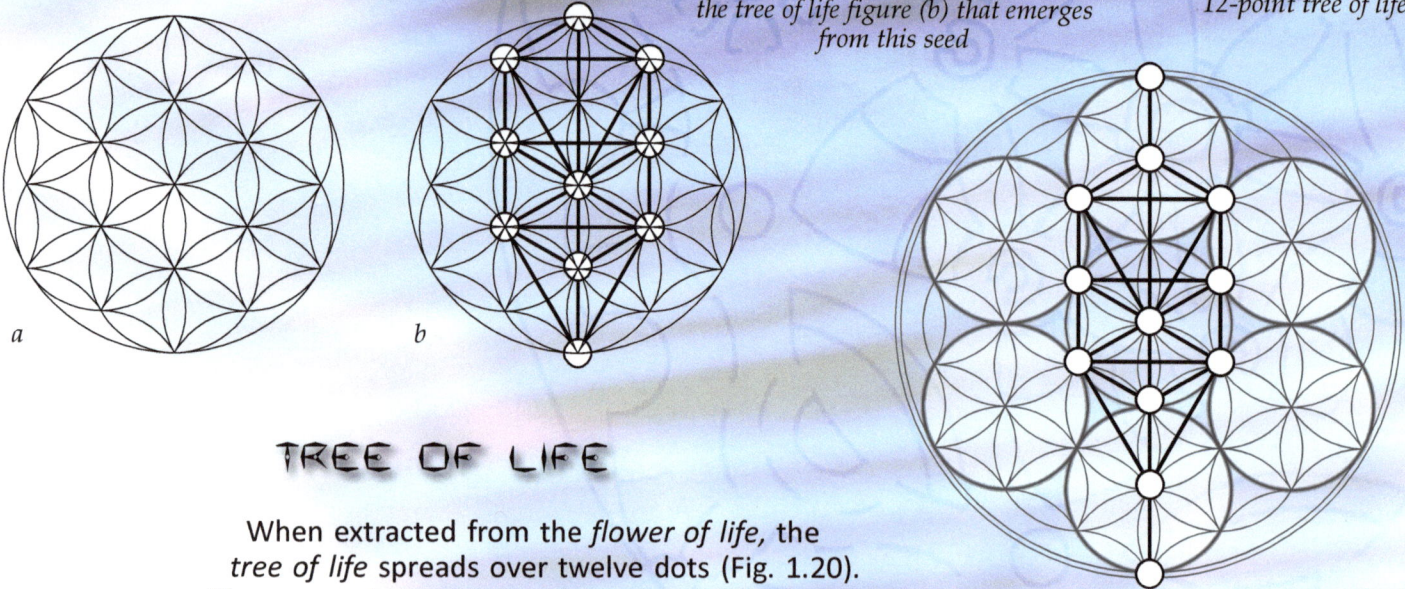

a

b

TREE OF LIFE

When extracted from the *flower of life,* the
tree of life spreads over twelve dots (Fig. 1.20).
There are also versions of the *tree of life* made of
thirteen dots.

In the Jewish mystical doctrine known as *The Kabala,* the *tree of life*
pattern is utilised to illustrate its theory of the ten creative forces that intervene
between the infinite, invisible, unknowable God, and our visible, created world.
The *tree of life* symbolises the map of the universe and psyche, and is seen as
the cradle of divine wisdom. It is a guide for self-understanding and for spiritual
enlightenment based on the reflection of the order inherent in the Cosmos.

Universal forces are constantly acting upon us so that a macrocosm is mirroring
itself onto a microcosm. This relationship between God and the human, the Divine
and terrestrial, is rightly represented by a tree. The tree is rooted in Mother Earth,
stabilised and nourished by her substance. From the root, its trunk rises towards the
sky and proliferates into the crown of branches, all serving to enable wider contact
with light. Light is another kind of food needed to sustain the life of a tree. This story
of the tree is a metaphor for the human being placed between *Earth* and the *heavens*
as a mediator, connector and the processor of these two forces.

By acquiring spiritual maturity and wisdom, a human comes closer to the *divine*. The
ten dots of the *tree of life* are ten spheres called the ten *sephirot* in Hebrew, and they
are like seeds that need to sprout on the spiritual path. Within the ten sephirot, five
are considered masculine while the other five are seen as feminine. Ten sephirot are
connected by 22 lines.

These lines symbolise active relationships between the *sephirot,* and each line is named after one of the 22 Hebrew letters. Since there are 22 geometrical solids composed of regular polygons (5 *Platonic solids,* 13 *Archimedean solids* and 4 *Kepler-Poinsot solids*) and 22 letters in the Hebrew alphabet, there is one regular solid associated with each letter and line.

This Hebrew wisdom has inspired many artists throughout history. Some of the greatest examples of the *tree of life*'s records in architecture are the floor plan of St. Paul's Cathedral in London, which is a clear replica of the *tree of life,* and the Church of St. Michael in Barje in Slovenia designed by the Slovenian architect **Josef Plečnik**[I-19] (1872-1957). Not only does **Plečnik**'s work feature the geometry of the *tree of life* on its main façade, but the entire building is based on *sacred geometry* pervaded with the measures/numbers originating from alphanumerical values of chosen words. It also incorporates symbols derived from various occult traditions.

FRUIT OF LIFE

When we add 36 whole spheres (18 blue + 18 grey ones; Fig. 1.23a) to the 19 whole spheres, which are the base of the *flower of life,* and include the 6 spheres (in bold) that are missing in the grey generation, we witness the emergence of a new geometrical pattern pregnant with information.

Then, by selecting 13 spheres, we get a figure called the *fruit of life* (Fig. 1.23b). This pattern is one of the most potent informational systems of Creation. It is a determiner of the geometry of both the animate and inanimate worlds.

Perfect TOUCHING ELIMINATES STORING OF INERTIA, AND PROMOTES PERFECT DISTRIBUTION…

Mother Nature gets her billiard balls touching perfectly. This allows an instant communion of the passage of waves of charge – creating a telephone network called LIFE.

Daniel Winter

▼ 1.22 – The number 61 (grey) is a centred hexagonal number, as are 37 (blue) and 19 (black). Figure 1.23a is made of 61 spheres (55+6).

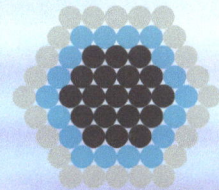

▲ 1.21 – The flower of life based layout of the 2nd floor of the Millennium Dome building in London (architectural design by Milena)

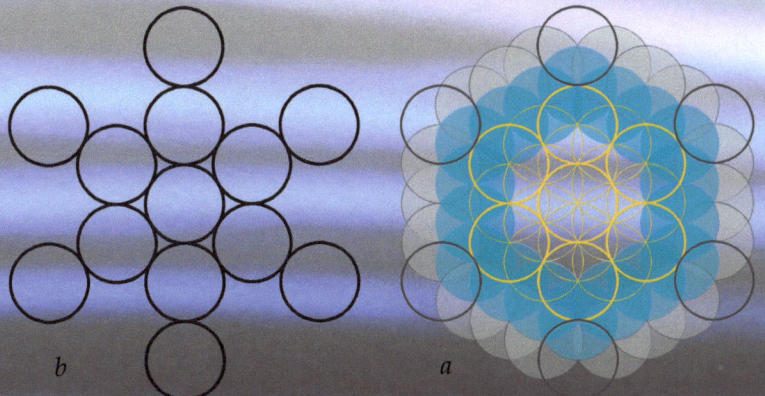

► 1.23 – The fruit of life, made of 13 spheres (b), and its geometrical origin (a)

b

a

14

◄ 1.24 – 'Flowers' – (Six around One)
ideal communication pattern between the layers of life.

*Any circle/sphere of this 'flower' can bloom a new
(Six around One) 'flower', and so on endlessly.*

*The substance of God is an ultimate model of fluid
interconnectedness and of perfect information transfer
within All That Is.
Only love can make such an immaculate touching.*

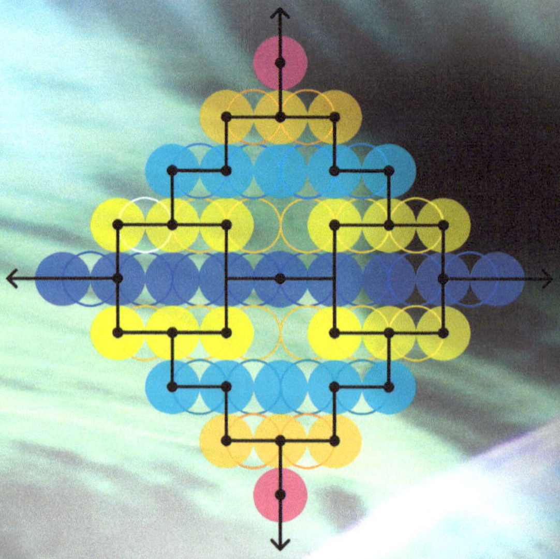

The *fruit of life* can also serve to illustrate the
inward and outward processes of Creation.
Since in every circle seven smaller circles of
the same radius can be perfectly inscribed,
it is possible to perform that process on any
circle within the *fruit of life* and thus start a
new generation of *fruit of life* patterns. Figure
1.27 illustrates this geometry which generally
can evolve in two directions: augmenting – if
we start from the pink figure, and diminishing
– when we begin with the grey *fruit of
life* figure. Both processes are potentially
everlasting.

Curved lines are associated with female
energy while straight lines are associated with
male energy. Also, females process magnetic
currents while males process electrical ones,
and hence feminine energy essentially has
magnetic properties as opposed to male
energy that is electrical in nature. The *fruit of
life* is composed solely of spheres and is seen
as a symbol of feminine creative principle.

METATRON CUBE

If we use the *fruit of life* as a starting ground, we can
draw straight lines connecting the centres of all thirteen
spheres with one another. The resulting geometry is a
symbiosis of female and male energy and is called the
Metatron cube (Fig. 1.25).

The *Metatron cube* is a geometrical pattern out of which
the *Platonic solids* emerge. They were known even to
the Neolithic people but were named after **Plato** who
believed that the world of atoms and the whole cosmic
realm were configured on these perfect forms.

Know one, know all.

Katha Upanishad[(1-20)]

► 1.25 – The Metatron cube,
*a pattern based on 13 spheres/circles of the
figure called fruit of life*

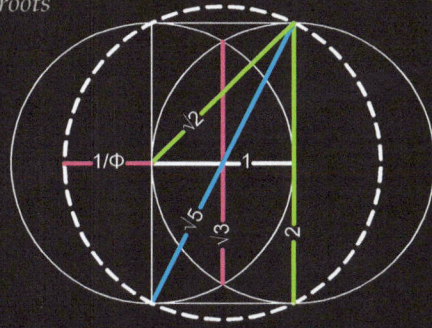

1.26 – The vesica pisces provides a geometrical illustration of the values of π, 1/Φ and the square roots of 2, 3 and 5

Platonic solids are archetypes of shapes that can be constructed in three-dimensional space. They are the only regular solids. That means they can be placed in a sphere where all of their vertices touch the surface of the sphere. Also, if the sphere is placed inside each *Platonic solid,* then the sphere touches the midpoint of each of its faces. All the faces of one *Platonic solid* are the same in shape and size, all of its edges are the same length and all of its interior angles between faces are the same. The *Metatron cube* contains the pattern that provides lines, as potential edges, for every *Platonic solid*.

Each *Platonic solid* has faces that are made up of an equilateral and equiangular polygon: *tetrahedron, octahedron* and *icosahedron* are composed of triangles, a *cube* of squares and a *dodecahedron* of pentagons. These polygons carry in themselves the properties of the numbers Three, Four and Five respectively, and were once the core of ancient Egypt's science and philosophy. Later on, Three, Four and Five were featured by *Pythagoras* as the whole-number illustration of his theorem. The number Six is a latent companion of this well known *Pythagorean triplet,* since it is the area of a triangle with sides three, four and five units long (Fig. 1.28).

Besides Three, Four, Five, the π – which resides in every circle or sphere, and the Φ – present in the pentagon/pentagram, there are some other numbers relevant to the family of the *Platonic solids*. These are: the square root of 2, the square root of 3 and the square root of 5. Apart from the numbers Three, Four and Five, the others are *irrational numbers* and we find them in the geometry of the *vesica pisces* (Fig. 1.26).

1.27 – The Metatron's cube self-propagation

1.28 – Pythagoras' triangle: the relationship between 3, 4 and 5

Through the history of mathematics, from as long ago as the 20th century BC in Egypt then Mesopotamia, India and China, this theorem[(1-21)], amassed several hundred solutions, but the first recorded abstract proof was attributed to Pythagoras by Cicero and Plutarch

The style of functioning of the Total and the Universal Ordinance is the projection of the same System on the smallest part, that is, on the Particle. The operational Ordinance of the Human Being, of the Cosmoses and of Nature is equivalent to the operational Order of the Atom.

By a formula repeated in everything, the Six is assembled in ONE and the One is connected to the One.

The Knowledge Book
(F32, p 515, par 3,4)

There are five *Platonic solids* plus the mother of them all – the *sphere*. The sphere is always looked at as a model of perfect form and of an absolute singularity beyond comparison. All other forms come from it but only the most regular ones within them can precisely and harmoniously nest back inside the sphere.

1.29 – Tetrahedron

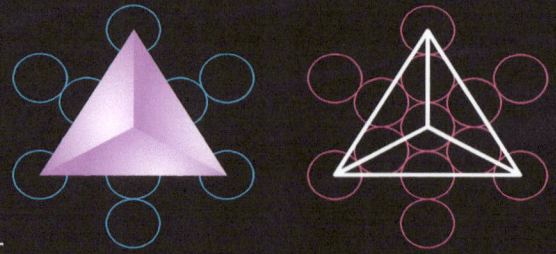

Compatibility with a sphere, as the *zero point* in Creation and a primal *Platonic solid,* is thus the criteria for determining the regularity of a solid. After the sphere, the first *Platonic solid* is a *tetrahedron* (Fig. 1.29). Four points only are enough to determine a tetrahedron, a solid which does not have diagonals. It is a polyhedron made of four equilateral triangles (*tetra* means *four* in Greek). Having four triangular faces, tetrahedron features a specific bond of the numbers Four and Three.

There is no simpler regular solid than the tetrahedron. If we inscribe all the *Platonic solids* into the same sphere, the tetrahedron is the solid which, with the greatest surface area, encloses the smallest volume within the circumscribed sphere, hence standing out as the best example of economy in spatial shaping. This property is the key of its toughness and stability – it is extraordinary rigid and the strongest of all the five *Platonic solids*.

Tetrahedral geometry is present in both the organic and inorganic world. The atoms of diamond molecules are structured purely in tetrahedral geometry which makes diamond the hardest known natural substance.

thymine
guanine
adenine
cytosine

The second *Platonic solid* is the *cube*. It is the most familiar solid of them all and is associated with the Earth, solid, and matter – as opposed to the sphere which is an archetype of the Source, Spirit and the heavens. A cube has eight vertices and its sides are made of six identical squares (Fig. 1.31).

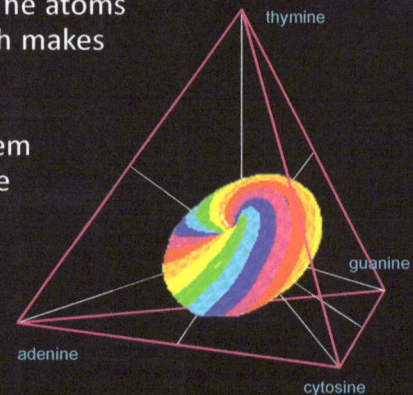

The third *Platonic solid* is the regular *octahedron* (*octa* means *eight* in Greek). This solid is made of eight equilateral triangles and it has six vertices (Fig. 1.32).

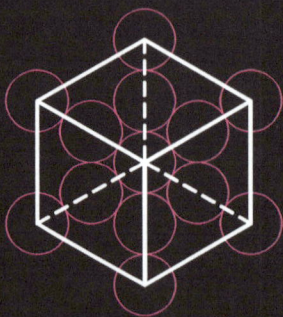

1.31 – Cube

The seven symmetry angles of a tetrahedron reveal a profoundly hidden 7-fold symmetry map on a spin-coupled toroidal surface. The tetra can be thought of as the sumtotal symmetry of mechanical principle. The toroid here embodies the transformation between the pure causal ('pure principle') and the mechanical phases of Creation. Their mutual (co-defining) physics can be thought of as the (only) sustainable symmetry of non-destructive charge interaction between the two. Together they form the general physics blueprint of all unit life (the esoteric 'Anu'); atomic, cosmic or biological, and more specifically that of conscious perception of a mechanical world.

Frank van den Bovenkamp
(Heart Coherence team)

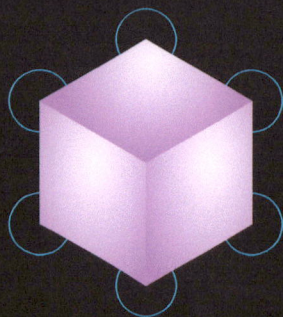

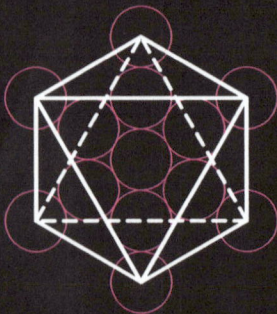

1.32 – Octahedron

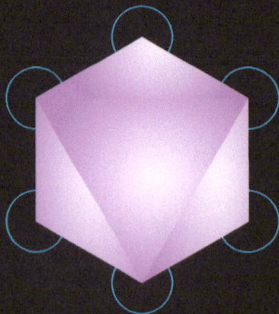

▲ *1.33 – Icosahedron*

▲ *1.34 – Dodecahedron*

▲ *1.35 – Star-tetrahedron*

The fourth *Platonic solid* is the regular *icosahedron* (*icosa* means *twenty* in Greek). The icosahedron has twelve vertices and twenty faces made of equilateral triangles (Fig. 1.33).

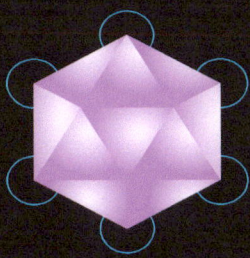

The fifth *Platonic solid* is the regular *dodecahedron* (*dodeca* means *twelve* in Greek) made of twelve regular pentagons with twenty vertices (Fig. 1.34). Its full name is the pentagonal dodecahedron and it is the solid volumetrically closest to the sphere. Due to that proximity to the unique excellence of the mother sphere, it is considered an all-encompassing form, which to the ancient Greeks represented a geometrical metaphor for ether and the Cosmos.

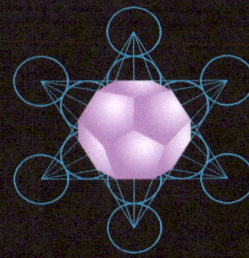

We owe the expression *quintessence* to these minds who, out of all the *Platonic solids*, revered the dodecahedron as a most special *(fifth)* being *(quintessence)* and the essence of the Cosmos. They promoted it into an entity which stood out from the other *Platonic solids*.

According to Greek mathematical philosophy, the *fifth being* exhibits the capacity of a cosmic embrace since it provides a nesting space for the other known elements.

The shape made of two tetrahedrons, called a *star-tetrahedron*, is inherent in the geometry of the *Metatron cube* even though it is not a *Platonic solid* (Fig. 1.35).

◀ *1.30 – What is biology? – illustration by Frank van den Bovenkamp*

Imagine that what we call 'biology' is the way the mechanical world invented how to build a toroidal charge vector thruster device using molecules.

Frank van den Bovenkamp (Heart Coherence team)

The dodecahedron occupies 66.49% of a sphere's volume when inscribed in it, while the icosahedron occupies 60.54%. Despite appearances, the dodecahedron is volumetrically closer to a sphere.

Every line of *the Metatron cube*, as an edge of a potential regular geometrical solid, represents a bridge between the visible and the invisible – a trajectory of the primordial life-force ready to appear as a perfect form.

The Metatron cube pattern is a precious piece of data from God's workshop.

It is a custodian of archetypal solids.

◀ *1.36 – Geometrical characteristics of the Platonic solids*

PLATONIC SOLIDS	Faces	Vertices	Edges	Angles
Tetrahedron	4	4	6	4x180°
Cube	6	8	12	6x360°
Octahedron	8	6	12	8x180°
Dodecahedron	12	20	30	12x540°
Icosahedron	20	12	30	20x180°
TOTAL	50	50	90	14400°

DNA is a four-dimensional Dodecahedron. This is a very loving embrace, and is the same for the 'dodecahedral' shape of the Earth Grid and Zodiac.

Daniel Winter

▲ *1.37 – The tetrahedron can endlessly reappear within itself, as a volume that is its own dual*

▲ *1.38 – The nesting of a tetrahedron inside a cube*

PLATONIC DUALS

All the *Platonic solids* exhibit a quality called *dualness*. The *dual* of a *Platonic solid* is another solid formed by having its vertices at the centre of each face of the parent *Platonic solid*. In other words, a *Platonic solid* has a dual when the number of its vertices is equal to the number of the faces of the other *Platonic solid* (Fig. 1.36).

The tetrahedron is the dual of itself since it has an equal number of vertices and faces (Fig. 1.37). It means that every tetrahedron is a nest of an infinite number of tetrahedrons: the process of connecting the midpoints of the faces of each newly emerged tetrahedron will endlessly generate new smaller solids, one inside the other.

The cube is the dual of the octahedron and *vice versa* (Fig. 1.40). The cube is also a perfect nest for the tetrahedron and can accommodate it in two different positions (Fig. 1.38 shows one of them). The dodecahedron is the dual of the icosahedron and *vice versa* (Fig. 1.41).

Each *Platonic solid* is potentially a nest to an infinite number of the *Platonic solids* of diminishing sizes and equally can be seen as a dual nested in a corresponding, bigger *Platonic solid* which is already nested in a yet larger one, and so on (Fig. 1.39). The endless inward and outward recursion, that these shapes are capable of, not only is the geometry behind spatial forms but, according to the latest scientific indications, of the phenomena of the inner world like self-awareness and consciousness.

The ancient Greeks believed that the *tetraktys* held the key of Creation and its inherent harmony. They found the ten dots, of their sacred symbol, also to be a blueprint for the geometry of the *Platonic solids*. Later on, **Johannes Kepler** suggested that the five *Platonic solids* perfectly fitted in between the six concentric spherical orbits of the six known planets of his time, thus determining the distances between the spheres (Fig. 1.42).

◄ *1.39 – The perfect harmony of the nested Platonic solids; starting from the biggest: cube (orange), tetrahedron (blue), octahedron (green), icosahedron (red) and dodecahedron (purple)*

The real Earth viewed from above is supposed to look like one of those balls made out of twelve pieces of skin sewn together.

Socrates[I-22]

▲ *1.40 – The dual relationship of the cube and the octahedron*

Besides this **p o l y h e d r a l h y p o t h e s i s** relating to planetary distances, **Kepler** introduced the sexual properties of these solids and devoted much time to analysing their relation to musical intervals. He attributed vertices of polyhedra with masculine nature and their faces with feminine. Following this premise, he divided the *Platonic solids* into *male* and *female* ones and derived dual connections between these two groups.

▲ *1.41 – The dual relationship of the icosahedron and the dodecahedron*

The primary group is made of the tetrahedron, cube and dodecahedron. All these solids have vertices common to the three faces and each solid is made of different faces: triangles, squares and pentagons respectively. In the secondary group are the octahedron and icosahedron. Both of them have faces made of triangles and vertices common to the four and five faces respectively.

According to **Kepler**, the dominant number between vertices and faces of one polyhedron would determine whether it belonged to the male or female family. The male polyhedra have more vertices than faces (cube and dodecahedron) while the polyhedra belonging to the female group (octahedron and icosahedron) have more faces than vertices. To marry one another, a given male polyhedron needs to have the same number of vertices as the female has faces. Thus, when one solid is nested inside another, there is one face per vertex and the female and male tokens are coupled.

▶ 1.42 – *Johannes Kepler's model of our solar system from his book*[1-23] *Mysterium Cosmographicum (1596)*

◀ 1.43 – *Each Platonic solid, nested in a sphere, is a nest of the other sphere into which a new Platonic solid can be placed, and so on. From left to right, the given nesting succession shows the cube, tetrahedron, dodecahedron, icosahedron, and octahedron. (Also see Fig. 1.42 and 1.44.)*

In *Platonic duals* **Kepler** t h e r e f o r e saw two notable marriages between the two groups of solids: of cube and dodecahedron, as males from the primary group, to female octahedron and icosahedron from the secondary group. The cube and octahedron, as well as the dodecahedron and icosahedron, are perfectly matching partners (Fig. 1.40, 1.41). The tetrahedron stands out as a hermaphrodite, self-sufficient and capable of nesting within itself (Fig. 1.37).

Cubic, cubeoctahedral and hexagonal symmetries appear in crystalline inorganic systems while the icosahedron, pentagon and its three-dimensional aspect the dodecahedron, are dominant in the geometry of living organisms and their growth.

Platonic solids illustrate the most economical use of space and are endlessly present in nature. Starting from the structure of atoms, DNA, and crystals, they guide energy and matter in shaping life forces into feasible and lasting forms. Amongst the forms only those which are able to perpetuate life charge are sustainable. Thus the process of sustainability is geometrically explainable and has to do with the ability to harmoniously embed: for waves – shorter waves into longer waves and for shapes – smaller shapes into bigger shapes. The *golden proportion* is the divine key to this process.

Volumes emanate their properties throughout space, ordered by the geometrical genius of the Creator. Engaged and seemingly empty space, the things we can see and those we cannot, are all part of a grand cosmic lace of astounding geometrical intricacy where One is experiencing itself as Many.

The Earth orbit is the measure of all orbits. Around of it, we circumscribe the dodecahedron. The orbit circumscribed around of the dodecahedron is the Mars orbit. Around of the Mars orbit we circumscribe the tetrahedron. The orbit circumscribed around of the tetrahedron is the Jupiter orbit. Around of the Jupiter orbit we circumscribe the cube. The sphere circumscribed around of the cube is the Saturn orbit. In the Earth orbit the regular icosahedron is inserted. The orbit entered in it is the Venus orbit. In the Venus orbit the octahedron is inserted. The orbit entered in it is the Mercury orbit.

Johannes
Kepler

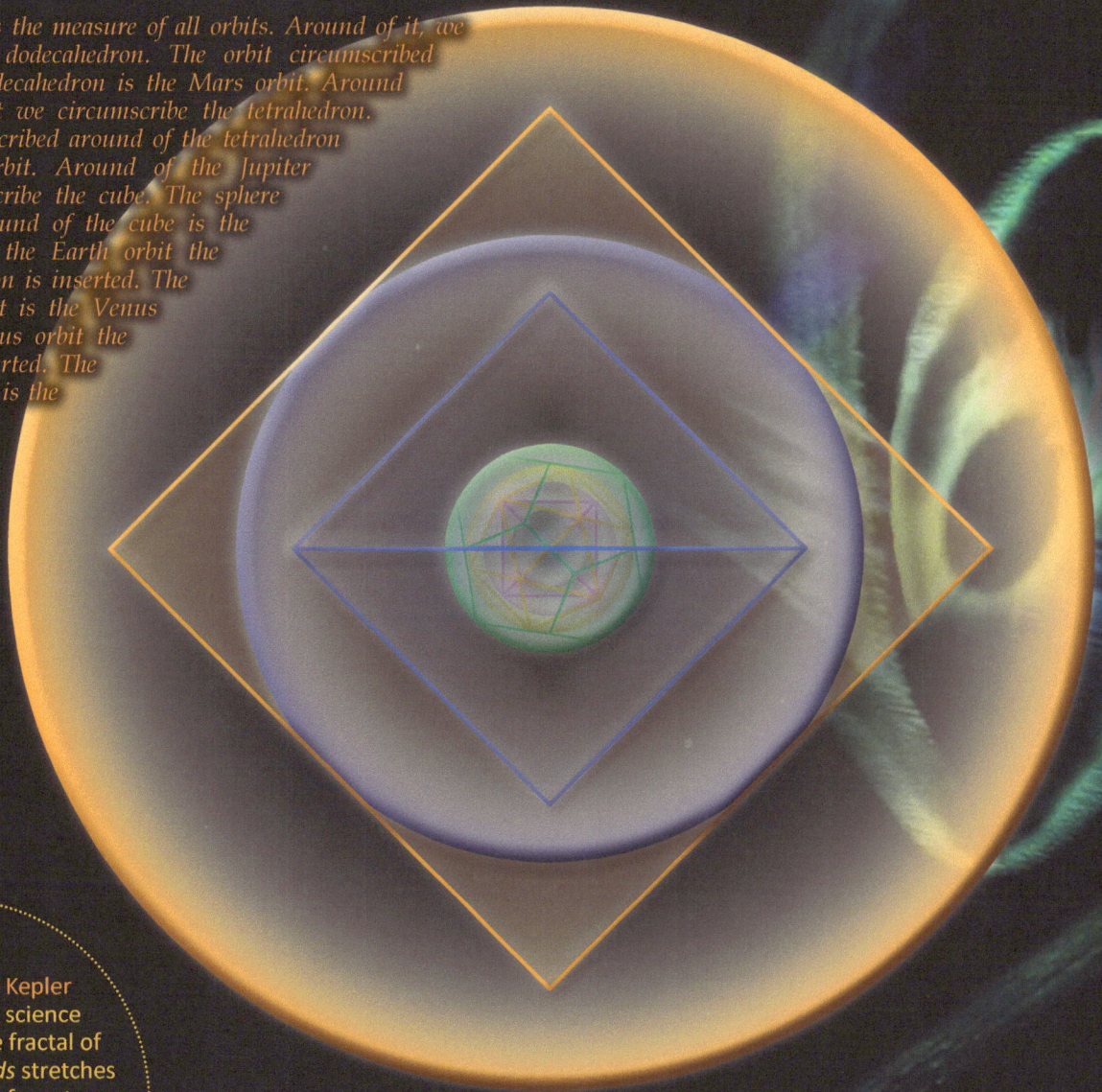

What Plato and Kepler intuited modern science has confirmed: the fractal of nested *Platonic solids* stretches from the structure of an atom, across the Earth's energy matrix to the realm of planets and their orbits. It establishes interdimensional order and harmony.

Re-member
that it is not about you.
It is about all of us.

The Group (through Steve Rother)

All right, what is the Human Being? The Human Being is the one who can Reach the Supremacy of being able to share the Consciousness of a Total.

Vedia Bülent (Önsü) Çorak (Light)

Each time you extend each edge of the dodeca straight out, by Golden Mean 'stellation', you make Icosahedron. Doing this again makes another dodeca... infinitely. This is the universe's only perfect three-dimensional wave fractal. This is the shape of DNA (ratcheting Dodeca), Earth Grid, and Zodiac (12 faced). This shape is variously called Merkabbah, Ezekial's wheels, City of Revelation, etc. Obeying this rubric made as above so below. And created image and likeness.

Daniel Winter

MUSIC
– DANCE OF INVISIBLE SHAPES

SOUND MADE VISIBLE

Sound is the first of three powers issued out of the primordial mysterious Point. With the appearance of *light* and *fire* the archetypal power-trinity was completed and the metamorphoses/reflection of these three equivalent initial powers allowed for the Creation process that has reached our time[III-29]. Sacred texts of both East and West explain the divine manifestation as a procedure that involves the unfolding of sound.

In the beginning was Brahman with whom was the Word. And the Word was Brahman.
Vedas

In the beginning was the Word, and the Word was with God, and the Word was God.
The Bible (John 1:1)

But His command, When He intendeth a thing, Is only that He saith unto it: 'Be!' – And it is.
The Quran (36:82)

Atum is by nature a musician Who composes the harmony of the Cosmos and transmits to each individual the rhythm of their own music. If the music becomes discordant, don't blame the musician.

Thoth[II-1]
(The Hermetica)

The validity of these ancient statements was assessed through acoustics, founded by the German physicist and musician **Ernst Chladni** (1756–1827).

Studying the structure and dynamics of waves and vibrations, in 1775 he performed an experiment: using a violin bow he caused a brass plate sprinkled with sand to vibrate. In response to the vibrations of sound, the sand repositioned itself producing patterns which later became known as *Chladni figures* (Fig. 2.2).

We rarely hear the inward music, But we're all dancing to it nevertheless, Directed by the one who teaches us The pure joy of Sun Our music master.

Mevlana Celaleddin-i Rumi[II-2]

Music is a secret arithmetical exercise and the person who indulges in it does not realize that he is manipulating numbers.

Leibnitz[II-3]

During the experiment the plate vibrated in a complex way with some parts staying motionless whereon sand gathered, after being shaken off the parts that were vibrating.

Chladni's research proved that sound affects physical matter: when the vibrating plate reached a point of resonance with the sound, the sand registered the energy pattern of the sound as a visible form, in this case two-dimensional. The three-dimensional geometry of sound was captured much later by the use of more advanced technology.

Hermann Helmholtz (1821–1894) was yet another German physicist who also experimented with musical instruments. He observed the way their sound would influence the sand and he recorded a series of interesting patterns. The Swiss scientist **Hans Jenny** (1904–1972) called this new area of research *cymatics*, after the Greek word *kyma (κύμα)* meaning *wave*. In 1950's he constructed an acoustic instrument called the *tonoscope* which enabled scientists to see the geometry behind the human voice for the first time.

From that moment on, it become possible to translate into a visible form not only the energy behind musical notes, played by a musical instrument or uttered by a human, but also the energy behind any song and vowel directly produced by a human, bird or another animal. These acoustic experiments have shown that audible vibration has its own visual energy pattern and is capable of structuring matter, which makes us think how even sound vibrations beyond our perceivable level can order matter into corresponding forms.

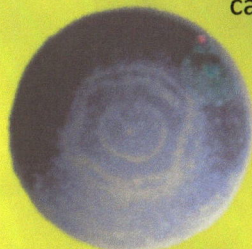

▲ 2.1 – Recorded by John Reid, CymaGlyphs make the geometry of sound visible: 1 – Blackbird; 2 – Dolphin; 3 – Flute; 4 – Sine wave; 5 – The word 'love'; 6 – The vowel 'e'; 7 – Tawny owl; 8 – Robin song

With the development of science, the meaning of sacred texts that the ancients recorded is gradually becoming clearer to us. For example, acoustic findings enable us to accept the ancients' belief in all Creation being the result of the Creator's emanating sounds while playing His eternal music. Even though we cannot hear all divine music, we now know that we can see one part of it with our own eyes.

Many cultures around the planet believed in a particular sound to be the primordial sound-signature of the entire Creation. According to Hindu tradition, it was *Om* (or *Aum*) and the god *Shiva* uttered it while creating the universe.

All sounds from nature contain beauty and embedded within them are many of the mathematical laws of the Universe. In the CymaGlyphs of humankind, apes, birds, dolphins, we see many mathematical constants, such as pi, phi and the fine structure constant, thus proving that all living things are connected to God.

John Reid[(II-4)]

Music has a more immediate connection with pure sensation than any other of the fine arts. – Helmholtz[(II-5)]

Amen (or *Ameen*) is the Christian sacred sound, *Hu* Sufis', while *Kung* (or *f*, or *f*-sharp) in China was considered the great tone of nature.

According to Hindu *tantric* tradition, *yantras* are seen as visual expressions of harmonies contained within sounds of corresponding *mantras*. *Cymatics* experiments have shown that the sound *Om*, correctly uttered, creates an image that resembles the geometry of *Sri yantra* — which is believed to keep the record of the primeval sound *Om*. From such findings, we understand how spiritual traditions deserve to be taken seriously. At the end of the day, what spirituality and science both try to explain are the same causes and powers that govern existence.

▼ 2.2 – Chladni's figures from his notebook – modern science can predict the resulting figures, even when using a combination of vibrational values to influence a given plate.

Sound may be generally defined as an impulse given by the air through the ears to the brain and blood and passed on to the soul; and the consequent motion, which starts from the head and terminates in the liver, is hearing.

Plato (Timaeus)

Music is an art of a very abstract and yet very direct engagement with the Divine. It is made up of harmonious combinations of sounds which unfold their shapes through space and time. Sound is one of the primal creative Powers and we can perceive only a limited range of its frequencies. Numbers are behind the sound, and consequently behind the music — its tones, scales, harmonies and rhythms. If we confine music into a man-made composition, we could then add that it comes from the soul of a composer.

The mathematical background of sound and music was intuited about two and a half thousand years ago. **Pythagoras**[II-6], who spent many years in Egypt studying its knowledge and was initiated in the Egyptian Temple Sciences, believed that sounds were emanated in a divinely harmonious way from celestial bodies, and he called them the *Musica Mundana (Music of the Spheres)*. He saw the Cosmos as a giant musical instrument that uses sound patterns to create, communicate and rule throughout the vast self. Thus, to him, this peculiar music regulates the rhythms and cycles of nature and man.

Jupiter	purple	DO
Moon	colourless light	RE
Venus	red	MI
Saturn	yellow	FA
Mars	orange	SOL
Mercury	green	LA
Sun	blue	TI

▲ *2.3 – The correlation between planets, colours and musical notes, made by the Ancient Greeks*

We shall therefore borrow all Rules for Finishing our Proportions, from the Musicians, who are the greatest Masters of this Sort of Numbers, and from those Things wherein nature shows herself most excellent and complete.

Leon Battista Alberti[II-7]

Different levels of energy interact through resonance to produce harmony… During resonance all the strings of similar quality in the universe interact. The change on each string is exchange of information, sensed as quality. We can not separate the physical form from the emotional or the mental levels of energy. The common factor between these levels is energy, which manifests differently on every level within us. But energy will also be affected by resonance with similar levels in our environment. These are what we call the collective levels. We are constantly affected by and in turn constantly affect the collective vitality, emotional, and mental abstract energy levels around us.

- Dr Ibrahim F. Karim

Since sound (music) translates into colour, music showers us with the colours of its sounds. On the other hand, silence is a medium of sounds beyond our perception therefore silence has its own colours. Ancient Greeks understood that the pulsating of the planets reflected colours, and that musical tones were just another form of colour (Fig. 2.3). The numerical properties of the orbiting relations of the seven celestial bodies around the still centre, which was than assumed to be the Earth, were considered an example of the perfect harmony of the heavens. **Pythagoras** believed that listening to these sounds would enable one to ponder upon the structure of the Cosmos and perceive its inherent beauty. He also thought that immaculate cosmic order was an ideal to be copied and strived for here on Earth. To him, musical instruments translate divine principles onto our level and contribute towards harmonising life.

GEOMETRY OF THE SOUND

To **Pythagoras**, who saw the origin of everything in numbers, the importance of music inevitably was connected to its numerical base. His admiration of numbers naturally developed into an interest in music, so he played many musical instruments and studied the physics of sound. As a result, **Pythagoras** mathematically defined notes — the ancestors of modern notes.

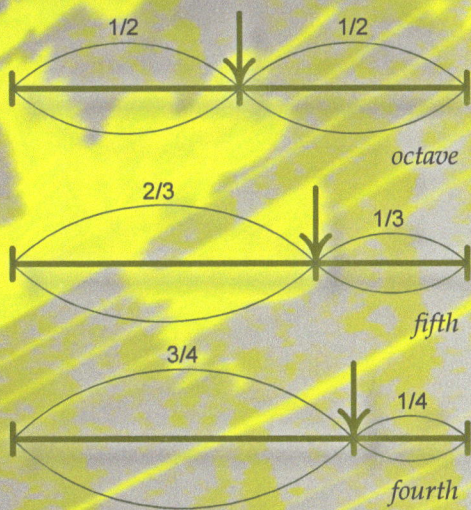

2.4 – *The geometry of the sound of an octave, a fifth and a fourth*

The ratios 1:2, 2:3 and 3:4 are also relations between neighbouring rows of tetraktys

First (unison).........................	1:1
Second.................................	9:8
Minor third	6:5
Major third	5:4
Fourth.................................	4:3
Fifth	3:2
Minor sixth	8:5
Minor seventh	9:5
Major seventh	15:8
Octave	2:1

2.5 – *Intervals, in modern major and minor scales, reveal the numerical nature of musical values*

2.6 – *The piano keyboard has eight white and five black keys within an octave.*
The octave (C-C) is divided into twelve equal semitones.

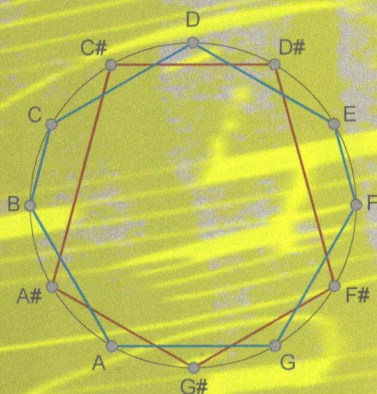

2.7 – *The symmetry of white and black notes reflects the harmonious relationship of Seven and Five within the octave of C-major*

In order to tune his lyre, he also identified three musically most significant intervals. One of the simplest definitions of a *musical interval* is that it represents the distance from one note to another, or is the ratio between the so-called *base note* and any other note. *Interval* is named according to the number of the notes included in it; like six – *sixth* or seven – *seventh*. **Pythagoras** noticed that, if the string was plucked at half its length, the sound produced would be eight notes higher (an *octave*) than the original sound produced by using the whole length of the string (2:1). Correspondingly, plucking at double the string's length produced the same note but an *octave* lower (1:2). Further on, by plucking the string at its 2/3, **Pythagoras** produced the *fifth* (a note five places ahead in the musical scale) and by plucking it at 3/4 of its full length, he produced the *fourth*. **Pythagoras** realised that he obtained the same musical results applying these ratios (2:1, 1:2, 2/3 and 3/4) to any instrument he tested (Fig. 2.4).

The first, eighth, and fifteenth white key on a piano sound differently, being an *octave* apart, but produce an equal qualitative effect on us (Fig. 2.6).
That is how we know they are the same notes. They exhibit sameness and difference at the same time, or harmonious unity of different terms. Quantity is meaningful and perceived only through its quality side, so every quantity eventually speaks to us as a particular quality. Music is a great example of this phenomenon.

Reflecting upon the musical ratios 1:1, 3:4, 2:3, 2:1, **Pythagoras** noticed that they are made of the numbers 1, 2, 3, and 4 (Fig. 2.4). This particular numerical series was highly significant to him and his followers. We have seen how they presented these numbers as a triangular glyph, made up of ten dots, called the *tetraktys* and how the equation 1+2+3+4=10 was the core of Pythagorean philosophy.

In his book *A Beginner's Guide to Constructing the Universe*, **Michael S. Schneider**[II-8] describes the geometry of a musical scale that results from self-replication of *vesica pisces* (Fig. 2.8, 2.9). The shape created through that process acts like an acoustic instrument. It shows us the connection between geometrical laws and *musical intervals*, and helps us to understand why the *vesica pisces* is considered the Mother of all shapes and sounds.

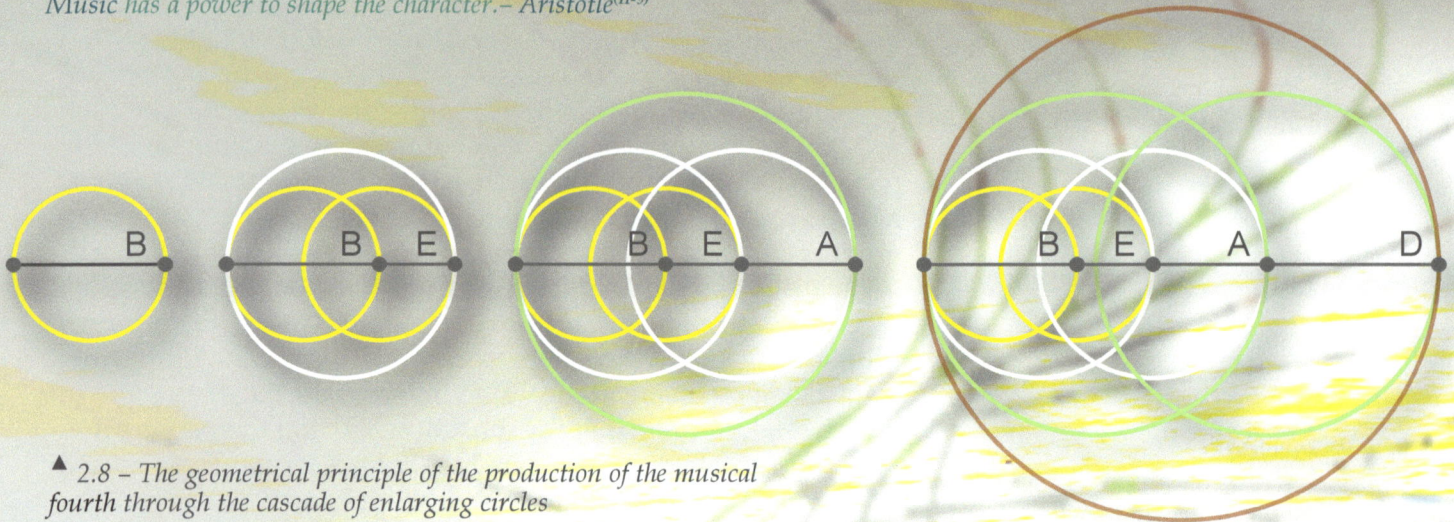

▲ *2.8 – The geometrical principle of the production of the musical fourth through the cascade of enlarging circles*

Looking at figure 2.8; if we assume that the diameter of the initial circle represents the length of a string, sounding the note B, then extending the length by 1/2 of the given circle's diameter will produce the note E, a musical *fourth* from B. With each step of an ascending process, this procedure will identify a note that is called a musical *fourth*. Looking in the opposite direction, descending by 1/3 of the initial biggest circle's diameter, the same geometry marks the notes which are a musical *fifth*. These two movements, which happen along the same notes, are equivalent: ascending by a *fourth* and descending by a *fifth,* and the other way round. In this example, the replication of the *vesica pisces* defines seven musical notes B, E, A, D, G, C, and F that span through three *octaves* (Fig. 2.9).

Music is a vibration and is therefore a form of vibrational communication. Music is not a human attribute, but rather, a spiritual attribute; therefore it runs by different principles than you experience in human form. It is for that reason that you have a separate part of your brain dedicated to interpreting and remembering vibrations in the form of music. As a young child you often memorize complicated things by putting them into musical form.

The Group
through Steve Rother

Music in its purest essence is as eternal as the soul and is an inherent ingredient of the energy of love – that's how important music is to ascension, or spiritual evolution. Not all sound that is proclaimed on Earth as music IS music! I'm not restricting compositions to a narrow band of 'masterpiece' musical styles, but rather I'm saying that piercing, clashing, raucous, dissonant sound is not music, it is noise. Those sounds fracture the body's energy, short circuit its electrical system, shatter its equilibrium, and prevent light from entering.

Matthew
through Suzanne Ward[(II-10)] *(Matthew Books)*

Music is the language of the heavenly hosts, and of the Angels, who are messengers of Divine Love and Will for the highest good of ALL.

Angels of Music – Soteri[(II-11)]

Music is a moral law. It gives a soul to the universe, wings to the mind, flight to the imagination, a charm to sadness, gaiety and life to everything. It is the essence of order, and leads to all that is good and just and beautiful.

Plato

I am convinced of the truth of Pythagoras' saying that Nature is sure to act consistently… I concluded that the same numbers, by means of which the agreement of sounds affects our ears with delight, are very same which please our eyes and our minds.

Leon Battista Alberti

Plato, who continued Pythagorean teachings, stated: *God, purposing to make the Universe most nearly like the every-way perfect and fairest of intelligible beings, created one visible living being, containing within itself all living beings of the same natural order*. This fractal order is based on harmonious interconnections of all elements, and reflects the perfection of God's way. Equally so, if we also follow the principle of harmony, our deeds will secure beauty both in terms of their function and their appearance. This alignment of two continuums, inner and outer, follows the universal laws of reflection and symmetry. Numbers and proportions are godly tools available in our world so that we can better understand and express timeless cosmic values.

With its three aspects: words, rhythm and tune, music for **Plato** was not only a means of earthly entertainment but a reflection of the harmony inherent in the laws of the universe. He was the one who stressed the power of music in influencing individuals and society: *when modes of music change, the fundamental laws of the state always change with them*. To him, the importance of a musical education was self-evident since it led to a proper practice of music and consequently to control of its tremendous power. *Musical training is a more potent instrument than any other, because rhythm and harmony find their way into the inward places of the soul* – he adds. Musical training in Plato's Academy included reading, arithmetic, painting and poetry, jointly called musical arts. It was suggested that music itself should be the first subject of education in the life of a child, followed by gymnastics to balance the development of the mind with the development of the body.

*There is geometry
in the humming of the strings...
There is music
in the spacing of the spheres.*

Pythagoras

The Geometry of Pressure in Your TOUCH predicts the Harmonics of EMOTION IN MUSIC and LOVE.

Daniel Winter

B E A D G C F

▲ *2.9 – Geometry, based on the expanding of the vesica pisces figure, shows the musical interval of the fourth (ascending from note B) and at the same time the interval of the fifth (descending from note F), through three octaves)*

On the other side of the globe, the Chinese scholar **Confucius** (c.551BC–479BC) had a similar concept of aesthetic education where he included six arts: music, calligraphy, mathematics, rituals, archery and riding. Music, an artistic subject such as poetry, dance, sculpture, painting and architecture, included other pleasure and joy-giving activities, like cuisine and hunting. *Be stimulated by Poetry, take your stand on the rites and be perfected by Music* – suggested **Confucius**.

The current names of the notes were chosen by **Guido d'Arezzo** (around 1000AD) as a reminiscence of cosmic entities and the eternal virtues associated with them. They are in Latin, and in his book *A Beginner's Guide to Constructing the Universe*, **Michael S. Schneider** provides the following table:

DO	DOminus	LORD	Absolute
SI	SIder	STARS	All Galaxies
LA	LActea	MILK	Milky Way Galaxy
SOL	SOL	SUN	Sun
FA	FAta	FATE	Planets
MI	MIcrocosmos	SMALL UNIVERSE	Earth
RE	REgina Coeli	QUEEN of the HEAVENS	Moon
DO	DOminus	LORD	Absolute

Music is a communication medium more potent than the semantic power of words and since ancient times it has been clear that music operates beyond the verbal domain. Seen that way, sounds are akin to colours except that, due to their fast movement through space, sounds make an immediate impact on the hearer. Our cells bathe in bliss, if the sound they are immersed in is well-suited to their frequencies and so can easily embed in our energy field. Music is therefore capable of taking us through very highly uplifting experiences of harmony, beauty, love, and unity with *All That Is*. Such is the healing and the therapeutic value of music.

SOUNDS AND COLOURS

Sounds and colours are among the most attractive tools of our creative expression. They are divine agents in our world. For as long as we are confined by this dense physical body, we cannot experience and convey their full potential since we are not able to hear all the infinite echoes of the heavens and see the colours beyond the rainbow. We perceive only those sounds and colours that are within the range of the frequencies compatible with our three-dimensional faculties. In order to have the perception of higher realities and to communicate with them, our thoughts would need to transcend the medium we live in. Such an achievement is a matter of consciousness' evolvement. By purifying ourselves through evolutionary challenges, we are advancing on that road.

Artists are capable of receiving the highest frequencies and, after processing them, through their artwork they offer them for the consumption of all. Frequencies of novelty spread that way are an evolutionary tonic for humanity. Visual artists have nature and all other visible forms to gaze at and to study, learn from, be inspired by or imitate. On the other hand, musicians that serve as focal points for capturing feelings, moods, melodies and rhythms of life, record the flow of energy and harmony behind the visible realm. They are mathematicians and physicists of the highest order for they decipher and deliver to us even the *music of the spheres* by processing it through their own essence.

Once created, sound lasts forever. It lives in silence which is its biggest strength.

Nikola Tesla[II-13]

I have discovered that all human evil comes from this man's being unable to sit still in a room.

Blaise Pascal[II-14]

Colour, which vibrates just like music, is able to attain what is most general yet most elusive in nature – namely its inner force.

Paul Gauguin[II-15]

The Sound of a blissful heart is music of implosion within, which is nothing but compression caused by braiding in your DNA and is a secret to how emotions program DNA.

Daniel Winter

LA Frequency is a Vibration accepted as a Unified titration of all Systems. This is a Frequency created by vibrations comprising various Colour and Sound tones peculiar to itself.

Frequency of the Spiral Waves is LA Frequency. This Frequency is a vibration assembling in a Totality the Ordinance of all the Cosmoses. LA Frequency is a Frequency of Existence.

The Knowledge Book (F35, p 575, par 1,2)

Since all artists translate the law of proportionality present in nature into various languages of their own expressive mediums, they educate people in aesthetic rhythms that are for the satisfaction and the nourishment of the soul. Musicians do it in a most explicit way. They make numbers flow through time providing a context of a unique kind for our entertainment and joy. Music, therefore, offers us an adventure: to experience ourselves in an inrush of invisible spatial shapes coming from the geometry of its sounds. When listening to music, we expose ourselves to change. Witnessing sounds that dance, merging with silence and with our being, we participate in the emergence of a new geometry around us, and consequently of our own energy field.

Music always works with silence by arranging its sounds around it thus activating the wholeness of being. Music enables both silence and sounds to express their best values by letting them interact together and portray one another. Every piece of music is a sound sample of the deep harmonies of life.

Silence is a divine substance and its geometry is more demanding than the geometry of audible sounds. An entire realm of sounds, undetectable to our hearing, lives in silence. To access silence and to stay in it, lots of self-awareness and self-love are needed. Courage is also welcome, because silence expands to infinity. Philosophers, scientists and artists are among those least uncomfortable with silence. Not only can they sustain its might, but they find a sanctuary in it. From their companionship with silence, precious divine gifts descend to our world.

This writing, as an arrangement of words, is ultimately a colourful picture – for words are vibrations with a colour value. If uttered, a word is an audible and thus a perceivable sound. In the case where it stays in our mind, a word is then a soundless sound, an internal colour. During our thought processes and verbal communication, we constantly paint a picture addressed to each other and to eternity. What an artwork we are entrusted to create by the very opportunity of living this life! If we choose our thoughts and speak our words with care, then the picture could become a glorious message of joy and gratitude to the Creator who has enabled our unique experiences.

You do not need to leave your room. Remain sitting at your table and listen. Do not even listen, simply wait. Do not even wait, be quite still and solitary. The world will freely offer itself to you to be unmasked, it has no choice. It will roll in ecstasy at your feet.

Franz Kafka[II-16]

DO
RE
MI
FA
SOL
LA
TI
DO
DO
TI
LA
SOL
FA
MI
RE
DO

Yellow is the lustre of the spirit.
Blue is the lustre of the soul.
Red is the lustre of the living.

Rudolf Steiner[II-17]
(Colour)

▲ *2.10 – Ascending and descending scales (8+8 notes=16) of an atomic whole – number Seven is the vibration of the sound frequency tonality of the atomic whole (1+6=7)[II-18]*

32

MESSAGES BEHIND SHAPES

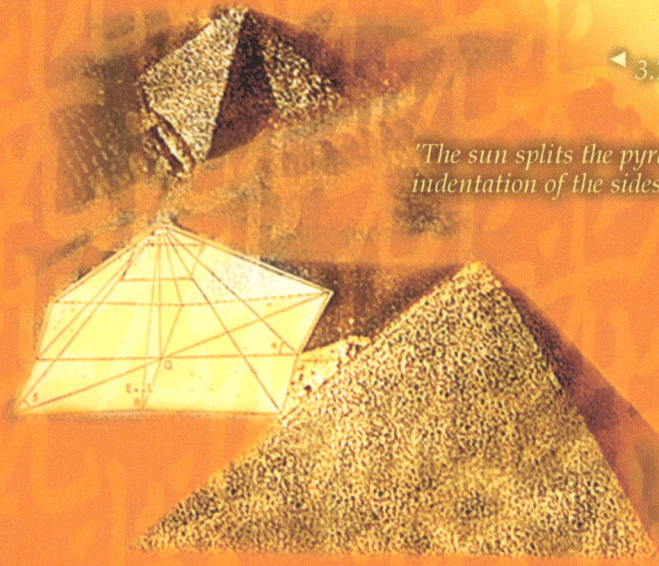

◄ *3.1 – The geometry of a pyramid*[III-1]
– a sun-enabled revelation

*'The sun splits the pyramid in two'. The secret lies in the
indentation of the sides. This is visible on the 21st March.*
– Dr Ibrahim F. Karim

Observations throughout the book so far have lead towards the assumption that everything has a shape and that shapes are geometrically definable. For example, we have seen how the language of fractal geometry is used to describe an inherent regularity within even 'formless phenomena' such as clouds, rain, noise, or awareness.

*With us, the name of every thing
is its outward appearance.
With the Creator,
the name of every thing
is its inward reality.*

Mevlana Celaleddin-i Rumi

Shape is not necessarily visible, but if we accept the premise that all is energy, then it is certainly an energy entity with a unique pattern. Consequently within the totality of energy, every thing is connected with every other thing and that continuous energy exchange is the essential nature of coexistence.

*The real voyage of discovery consists
not in seeing new landscapes,
but in having new eyes.*

Proust[III-2]

As an expression of their energetic signature, shapes take on an appearance related to the dimension in which they are present, be it in the realm of the physical, emotional or mental, or in the world of colour, sound, touch, smell and taste. All these aspects of existence talk to one another through the language of quality.

*Who has seen the wind?
Neither you nor I,
But when the trees bow down their heads
The wind is passing by.*

Christina Georgina Rossetti[III-3]

How does this ongoing communication between shapes affect human, animal, plant and other energy systems? The answer to this question is offered by *BioGeometry*™[III-4].

*The energy qualities produced through the use of BioGeometry have
the same vibrational quality components as sacred power spots.
BioGeometry actually transforms the energy quality of space to
produce a sacred power spot. This is the energy quality associated
with all spiritual activities, and is the main criteria in
Sacred Geometry and BioGeometry, as used in Architecture
from ancient civilizations down to recent times.*

Dr Ibrahim F. Karim

BioGeometry is a new scientific discipline formulated after 30 years of study and research by the Egyptian architect **Dr Ibrahim F. Karim**. *BioGeometry* is contained within, what **Dr Karim** calls, *the physics of quality. When nature recognizes quantity, it does so by interacting with the 'qualitative aspect of quantity'. In nature, for example, every number has a vibratory quality that can be transmitted through interaction and can produce effects on other energy systems* – notices **Dr Karim**.

BioGeometry deals with the energy of shapes by observing their interactions based on the principle of resonance. It focuses on deciphering the language of nature, expressed through the variety of shapes available to our perception. **Dr Karim** believes that understanding natural energy and its flow would help us to interact in a better way both with nature and between our own selves, which will serve to restore overall harmony.

BioGeometry identifies, but does not create, the energy signatures of shapes and applies its findings to inducing balancing effects in the energy of all living systems. In that process of balancing, the shape of an object is just a carrier of *BioGeometrical* energy that makes changes in the targeted energy field of humans, plants, animals, or environments. To produce desirable vibrational qualities *BioGeometry* also uses motion, orientation, colour and sound as its design language.

The universe will be found to operate on geometric intelligence primarily – this is the universal language. It is a frequency-coded universe, an information system. Thus shape of energy, plus frequency and dimensions, determines information.

Dr Noel Huntley[III-5]

▼ *3.2 – A ring engrafted with the wisdom of ages – the BioGeometry design*

PERFECT BALANCE

There are three vibrational qualities, recognised by *BioGeometry*, that shapes need to emanate in order to support a balanced and nurturing energy environment. These are: *negative green, a higher harmonic of gold and a higher harmonic of ultra-violet.*

According to **Dr Karim**, a shape is called *BioGeometrical* only if it produces these three qualities, and a system is in perfect balance only if it possesses all of these three components. *Negative green,* as a vibrational quality in resonance with grey, is the most important component in balancing so called spiritual energy and it is also *the core of all energy centres in the body and power spots in nature. Pyramids and hemispheres produce this vibration along their axis. In the spiritual energy field however, only the horizontal component of negative green is found; the vertical component, which is the harmful part of this energy, is cancelled*[III-6].

Energy entities are evolving personalities wherever they are nested in the grand fractal of life. Within that whole, *similar shapes enter into resonance with each other*[III-6]. This fact is the key to understanding the communication and transfer of information from entity to entity, or from level to level. Resonance provides the medium in which even opposites can become complementary.

If resonance occurs when similarity of shape exists, in order to influence a shape, its replica needs to be produced. *BioGeometry* focuses on finding out the energy signature of a given shape and on preserving that signature through its own design. The geometry of shapes, reduced to pure energetic parameters, has the ability to preserve the information and deliver the message of the whole shape. Only then is it possible to induce a desirable change through the virtue of self-similar shapes that are able to recognise one another and to communicate by establishing mutual harmony through resonance.

Furthermore, *BioGeometry* has produced evidence of the interchangeability of qualitative states. If, for example, the colour red is used as an energy carrier of information, its particular vibrational quality can be found in the sound behind the note *do (C)* or in any other sensory-scale. This means that any colour can be translated into a corresponding musical note as well as into qualities of fragrance, touch, taste or shape. In other words, colour, sound, smell, touch and taste can be represented as shapes, or subsequently as movements. This transformation is enabled by the continuity of vibrational qualities existing throughout the universal scales. *BioGeometry* stresses that quality is just a vibrational cipher of universal properties locked into particular frequencies that flow through the river of life.

▼ 3.3 – When the past speaks to the present through the language of shapes – design by BioGeometry

APPLICATION OF BIOGEOMETRY

The *physics of quality* provides the tool that modern technology needs in order to produce devices which support the prosperity of humans and the environment. *BioGeometry* offers holistically inspired solutions for a positive change towards balancing energy systems in numerous areas like architecture, the design of furniture, clothes, cutlery, crockery, gadgets, computers, transportation vehicles and mobile phones, the production of cosmetics, pharmaceutical drugs and medicines, and the raising of animals and the growth of plants.

We mistake outward appearance for totality, effect for cause. What we actually see are the external shells of manifestation, what is left by the formative energy. We don't see the energy that created the organism.

Alick Bartholomew (Hidden Nature)

3.4 – A holiday resort designed on principles of BioGeometry by the architect Dr Ibrahim F. Karim

BioGeometry in architecture was first applied in the design of 22 residential units of the first stage of the Old Vic resort in Hurghada, on the Red Sea in Egypt, built in 1984

View from the beach

3.5 – A BioGeometrically inspired shape

Research results have been monitored over thirty years and have proved that the application of *BioGeometrical* knowledge can protect us from various harmful effects of electronic equipment, Earth's radiation and other negative influences.

SILENT SOUND

The purpose of energy coming into existence is encoded in its shape. Geometry keeps a record of these shapes, whether or not they are perceivable to our senses.

BioGeometry has developed the concept of *silent sound* and defines it as a transformation of *BioGeometrical* architectural space, *BioGeometrical* shapes and patterns, *BioGeometrical* colour placements, *BioGeometrical* motion and body postures or *BioGeometrical* sacred tongue movements, into sound frequencies outside the audible range, recorded and replayed through digital media.

The idea behind *silent sound* is to reproduce the perfect harmony of all energy functions of life by bringing into the environment the main quality of *BioGeometry.*

Silent sound works as an agent in balancing the energy of humans, animals, plants and inanimate matter in its surroundings. Since it is inaudible, it can be played in the background with any other music in the home, car, airplane and even during sleep – possibilities are endless, explains **Dr Karim**.

BioGeometry devices and designs transform the energy of space and give it a quality associated with the sacred – similar to the effect that church bells, prayers from holy books or some other religious chants produce. *Silent sound* is a factor that balances energy when added to many products like mobile phones, computers, or used during television, musical, engineering and agricultural production. Unnoticeable, it serves the same purpose when released into the environment, be it the home, or a sporting or work place.

The use of *silent sound* has promoted a brand new way of enhancing the quality of life.

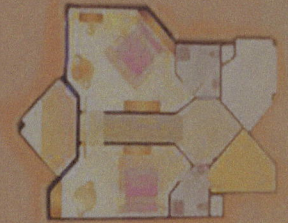

First floor plan

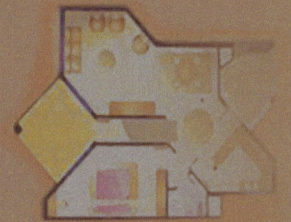

Ground floor plan

Sacred Geometry gives you the opportunity to take a BIG PICTURE look at yourself and your place in the world. Once mastered, it can be applied to healing, counselling, bio-feedback, researching, teaching, designing and the creation of PEACE, BLISS and ONENESS.

Daniel Winter

BioGeometry
is a pioneering effort to
scientifically explain the working of the
invisible by studying the interaction of shapes
displayed in the gallery of life and it is putting its
findings into a positive practice for the betterment of all.
Although innovative in one way, in another it actually reconnects
with the knowledge of ancient science from the time of the early
Egyptian culture. Thus, we all witness the principle of continuity as
resonance of vibrational qualities throughout the ages.

COOLING DOWN TO SEE PATTERNS

On the other side of the globe, in Japan, **Dr Masaru Emoto**, intrigued by water, has conducted numerous researches in order to get a deeper understanding of its nature. The results of his discoveries were first published in the book *Messages from Water*.

Dr Emoto started his experiments with the premise that water changes its quality according to the information it receives. Regardless of whether it comes from a voice, music, thought, noise, or a written word, information is always a particular vibration of energy. Everything is alive, if seen as energy, and everything communicates with everything since energy constantly moves. **Dr Emoto** uses the term *hado* for energy inherent in all things.

Water is a very absorbent medium and responds to its environment.
It may sound odd at first, but to respond to an influence is just
a manifestation of the continuous natural tendency towards
balance on all levels, understood and explained by physics and its
many laws. We are made of 70% water. If anything, in a material
sense, we are water in fact. Interestingly, about 70% of the
surface of the planet Earth is also water. With this in mind, **Dr
Emoto** wondered whether the key to understanding ourselves
better, and our Mother Earth, is to know more about our prime
bodily ingredient.

Dr Emoto studies water by taking samples, freezing them
and observing the way they crystallised. Since
there are no two identical snowflakes, for
him that is a sign of each snowflake
carrying unique information as an
individual response to the influences
it is exposed to. Thus he believes
that each sample of water, just like a
snowflake, contains authentic data.

*Feelings are
the attractive
magnetic force
of the universe.
The most
powerful feeling
is LOVE.
The mind is
the air element.
Feelings are the
water element.
The mental
understanding
that all life is
connected as a
web of energy
that mutually
sustains itself
becomes the
feeling of
LOVE in the
heart. Strong
flowing feelings
of LOVE are
the greatest
MAGNETIC
POWER to
attract and
materialize
perfection in the
physical world.*

*Angels of Love
(Miracles –
Afrei[(11-11)])*

▲ 3.6 – *Every shape is a message
carrier
– the BioGeometry design*

▲ 3.7 – *A BG cube
(BioGeometry device)*

According to Dr Emoto's findings, *love* and *gratitude* were messages, placed on water bottle labels, to which the water from the bottle responded by producing most beautiful crystals. All other information it received, even of a similar nature, did not result in so clear and perfect a shape of crystal. Dr Emoto also witnessed water consistently responding to positive words *(thank you, well done, angel, happiness)* by forming regular crystals, while when exposed to negative words *(you fool, no good, devil, unhappiness)* water was either not forming crystals at all, or they were broken or unbalanced.

Figures 3.7, 3.8, 3.9 illustrate the teamwork of **Dr Ibrahim F. Karim** and **Dr Masaru Emoto**.

Dr Emoto explores the effects of different energy qualities and captures them in the shapes of water crystals while **Dr Karim** uses shapes to produce harmonising energy qualities applicable to the environment.

It appears as if the energy behind words with a negative connotation exhausts water, and it is then not able to perform at its best by structuring itself into regular patterns of perfect crystal forms. Therefore, what we perceive as beauty seems to be the result of energies of a higher power, of benevolence, goodness, love and compassion. They spread throughout Creation by mirroring their own harmonious properties and manifest immaculate order and symmetry, adding value to whatever they come across.

If information which water is exposed to makes an impact on it, and since there is a clear regularity in water's response with regard to the type of the given message, it means that feeding water with controlled information will produce a desirable result. In other words, the quality of water can be manipulated in a predictable manner by the energy directed to it. **Dr Emoto** supposes that the same can also be extended to us.

Given the nature of its energies, the information we open ourselves to will inevitably influence our energy field and have a direct impact on our wellbeing. Thus, not only is it important to understand our ability to influence the way the water we use affects us, but to realise that we can help ourselves by monitoring and selecting the information we expose ourselves to during the day.

Dr Emoto's experiments demonstrate how naturally we can make changes in water, simply by sending it the message we want. Biologist **Dr Stanislav Zenin** arrived at the same conclusion. Scientific studies of this Russian Academician proved that water has memory and can be influenced by our words and emotions.

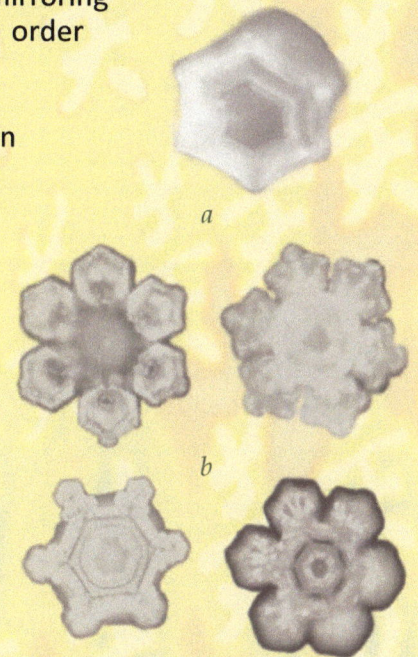

a

b

3.9 – Sample of the frozen tap water (a) and the same water after its exposure to the BG devices (b). The regular crystals illustrate the power of BioGeometry.

He engaged some healers and psychics in his research and discovered that water changed after being exposed to their thoughts. That ability of water he attributes to its molecular structure, which is suitable for storing information.

According to **Dr Zenin**, water possesses short-term and long-term memory. His findings showed that the short-term memory is a reversible change, while the long-term memory produces permanent changes in water's structure and comes as a result of long exposure to information.

The sending of love and gratitude works best for water and, according to the findings of **Dr Emoto** and **Dr Zenin**, it is ever so logical to assume that the same applies to us, humans. Water showed how *beauty* and *love* are carried and expressed through the most perfect geometry.

FORMULA OF LIGHT

In his experiments, **Dr Emoto** was able to see that water even 'understands' different languages. No matter from which language the expression *thank you* came, water would read its energy and respond in the same way. This fact indicates that, regardless of the language it is expressed through, words with the same meaning have equivalent energies. This finding leads to a conclusion that there exists another energy/power/force, however we name it – a carrier of meaning delivered from the same primeval source. Frequencies that carry meaning do not appear to be altered by the individual frequencies of the letters found in a word. This observation brings in a less explored dimension of words which the Serbian scientist **Spasoje Vlajić**[(III-7)] has been focused on.

While studying causal relations between the sound of a word, its colour state and its meaning, in 1984, **Vlajić** came up with a mathematical formula for expressing words as frequencies of colours, thus revealing their origin linked to archetypal values preserved in cosmic archives of light. This formula, which **Vlajić** named the *formula of light,* also shows the way the energy of a sound transforms into finer charges of nerve impulses and meanings. Using the frequency value of each letter in a given word, with the *formula of light* we can find the light-state of any word in either the Serbian language, or German, that **Vlajić** analysed.

For when we ourselves experience the life of colour, we step out of our own skin and take part in cosmic life. Colour is the soul element of nature and of the whole cosmos, and we have a share in this soul element when we experience colour.

*Rudolf Steiner
(Colour)*

According to the formula of light, the frequency of the word denoting a primary colour (blue, red and yellow) in the Serbian language equals the frequency of the colour it signifies. This means that the sum of the frequencies of the letters, used to spell the word red, gives the frequency of the colour red. The same principle is valid for the words blue and yellow.

Focused on the research of the natural relationship that exists between energy (sound, electromagnetic waves) and information (meaning), **Vlajić** also formulated a new discipline. He called it *Light Algebra (which) suggests solutions for the transformation of the system of decimal numbers into a system of coloured signs, as well as solutions for performing basic numerical operations in colour terms*[III-7].

The fact that besides their sound values our words carry a meaning, as vibrational information that gives them an essential quality, has led **Vlajić** to recognise a force working behind this phenomenon. He understood it as a *fifth force* in line with the four existing forces that modern physicists work with. These four forces *(gravity, electromagnetic, the weak nuclear force* and *the strong nuclear force)* behave in a cause-effect manner in the space-time dimension where the fastest speed is the speed of light. On the other hand, the *fifth force*, which he introduced and named the *force of meaning,* works through super-causal mirroring in a non-logical fashion.

This informational force is responsible for creating an overlapping of mental pictures and physical events which share the same meaning. Since **Vlajić** sees the attraction between thoughts and matter functioning above logical context, he connects it to performances of the right brain hemisphere. **Vlajić** believes this hemisphere links us with the primeval energy behind all things and all beings, and complies with the order of our thoughts. His language studies revealed that light transfers meaning, and though it lives through a sound, word, or form, meaning permanently remains the property of light. To him, light is a spiritual archetype. As such it is an indispensable tool of the divine creative intelligence.

Vlajić conducted computer studies of the first five chapters of *Genesis* from *The Bible* then studied *The Quran, The Kabala,* Far Eastern philosophies and various occult literatures to find regularities in the connection between the phonetic form of a word and the way its meaning is shaped, perceived and spread. For example, his analysis of the Biblical verse *In the beginning God created the Heavens and the Earth* revealed a frequency distinction between the words that relate to the Heavens and those pertaining to Earth. Two archetypal polarities were determined by the energy behind these words. Notions like *sky, Spirit, soul,* have frequency values of the colour blue while *Earth, mother, matter, man,* belong to the red-yellow frequency range.

▲ *3.10 – Light is an electromagnetic wave and the colour of it is determined by its wavelength. Visible colours, from red to violet, appear between 740 and 380 nanometres on the line of the electromagnetic spectrum which stretches from Gamma to Radio waves. (also see Fig. 3.23).*

This division also applies to words which describe qualities or positions in space: *light* (in weight), *gas, cold, that, there,* are all blue while *hard, strong, hot, this,* are of the red/yellow spectra. Further analysis of opposite pairs of words, with a good-bad polarity, has revealed regularity even in the appearance of certain letters. For example, some letters are more recurrent in words with a positive connotation while some are found more frequently in words of a negative connotation.

Vlajić's research shows that the primal conceptual division, indicated in the holy books by the words *the Heavens* and *Earth,* is conceived and present on the level of light and that it is energetically reflected in numerous words grouping them meaning-wise around these two archetypes.

THE COLOUR OF YOUR NAME

The *formula of light* unites sound, colour and number, revealing the light/colour properties that words bring into our life. Studying the frequency values makes it clear that light is a common denominator that connects the physical/physiological and the mental/spiritual continuums. Coming from that eternal and infinite field, information coded in the form of letters or words projects frequencies of its own dimension.

Consequently, some words emanate extremely high frequencies of their source. Thus by invoking the names of **Jesus Christ** or **Allah,** or some other sacred words, we usher in strong benevolent energies. The multiple names of God, given in holy books, might be particular formulae of vibrational healing and protection. According to **Vlajić**'s *formula of light,* the name of Jesus Christ in Serbian carries frequencies of a golden-yellow colour while purple is radiated from the words God and Allah. The word MEMENTO, for example, has the frequency of the yellow-green colour. Have you ever wondered what colour your name is?

THE WAY OF WORD

All sacred books come from the Cosmos as a training programme for humanity, to accustom us to the energies of the dimensions they originate from and to enlarge our cerebral potential. Religious fulfilment therefore means saturation with energies of religious books. Alphanumerical analyses of *The Bible* (**Richard Amiel McGough**) and *The Quran* (**Dr Rashad Khalifa**) indicate their celestial origin by showing them to be mathematically-composed literary works, far too complex to be attributed to the mind of a human from this planet.

The sacred books are given to us to advance our energies which are set onto the road of evolution. That task was programmed by numerical combinations behind the intricate nature of their texts. Hence numbers are used to convey values chosen by divine realm. They deliver the cosmic information contained in light. Access to that information is provided by letters, and our engagement with them activates the holy treasure of these scriptures.

If you ask Me anything in My name, I will do it.

The Bible (John 14:14)

Do you not see that GOD has cited the example of the good word as a good tree whose root is firmly fixed, and its branches are high in the sky? – The Quran (14:24)

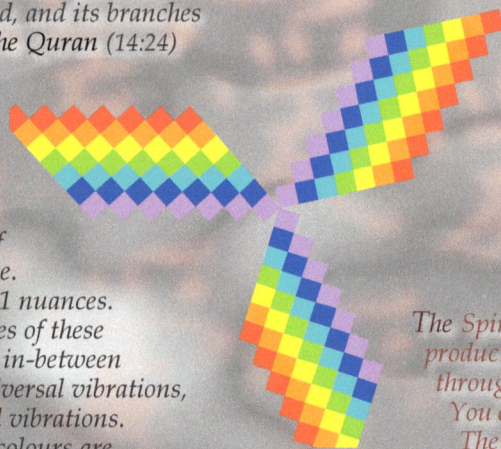

3.11 – *147 colours of the divine kaleidoscope. Each colour has 1001 nuances. The sound tonalities of these colours and their in-between tones create universal vibrations, that is – spiral vibrations. The first 49 colours are divine waves. The second 49 colours are celestial waves. The third 49 colours are the mirror of truth* (III-8)

The Spiral Sound Vibrations are healthier and more productive than direct Vibrations. The Sound issuing through Breath can only be heard on Earth. However, You can never hear the Secret Language of Your Cells. The one who knows how to Master his/her Voice also knows how to Master his/her Body.

When the Sound Vibrations the Cells can Perceive are, one by one, Unified with the Sound Speeds of the Cells, each Cell melts down with that Sound. Each Cell which melts down possesses the Consciousness of the Universe at that moment. For this reason, it Unifies the Cellular Vibrations with those Speeds of Sound in each Medium it goes to and completes its Body.

The Knowledge Book (F54, p 948, par 5,6)

MESSAGES BEHIND SHAPES

By reading sacred books and copying them in our own handwriting, through centuries we have been pondering deeper and deeper into their energies. Those efforts have been strengthening our cerebral apparatus while our consciousness has gradually expanded. Consequently, the process of enlightenment enabled us to better communicate with our soul.

The holy books therefore have made us into who we are today, by the emanation of their light through words of all languages. They have been purifying us with the power of the energy of the dimensions they came from, thus working on our genetic potential. Influenced by that divine word-number matrix, human consciousness has opened further on to light. And now, each new day, every one of us can shine more, coming closer to fulfilling our cosmic destiny of returning to the stars.

The aim is to shine with the brightest of all lights. Its name is *conscious love*.

Equipped with our religious heritage, we can speed up that process now. If the meaning of our thoughts, feelings and words is positive and if we see, support and invite unity, we will accelerate our transformation into brighter beings. That glow will reflect itself wherever we go, onto whatever and whoever we meet.

Everyone
Is God speaking.
Why not be polite
and Listen
to Him?

Hafiz[(III-9)]

ALLAH
is a Totality of neutral Con-
sciousness that contains all knowledge and ener-
gies in itself. If we visualise an egg, the shell is then Atlanta
Dimension. The membrane beneath is the final boundary of the Di-
mension of Truth, that is of the All-Truthful's Dimension, while the in-
visible energy totality between the shell and the membrane is the Totality
of Consciousness. Energy that he attracts from the Totality of Conscious-
ness, the All-Truthful projects onto the Dimension of Allah (O).
The egg white is the sum of all dimensions of the All-Truthful
and the egg yolk is the sum of all Gürz crystals[(III-10)].

A T L A N T A DIMENSION

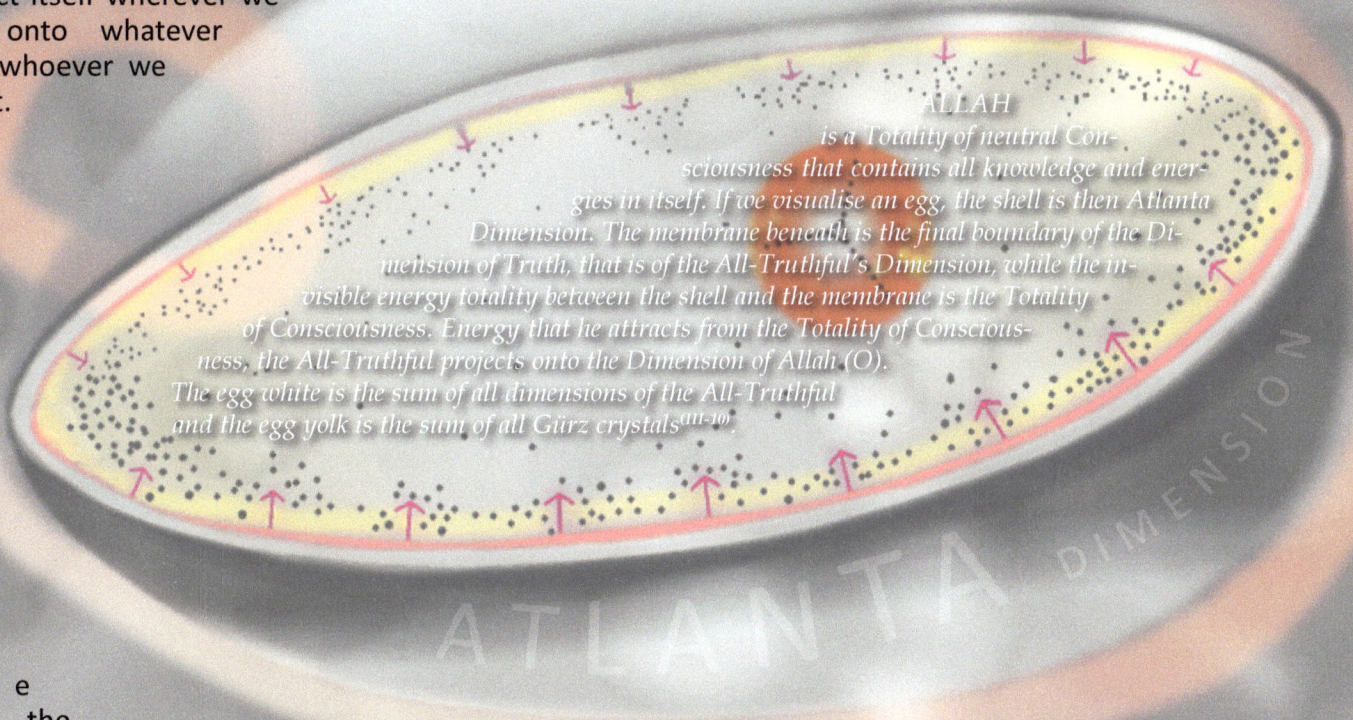

One of the links with our celestial home has been maintained through the energy of the holy books. Captured by numbers, the divine rhythm that echoes through them has been animating and guiding us for centuries. However, when every cell of our body knows how to dance to it, and gets saturated with it, we inevitably start looking for a new frequency range to nourish and to inspire us. Thus the meaning and joy of life are maintained.

The stars are
God's dreams,
thoughts
remembered
in the silence
of the night.

Henry David
Thoreau[(III-11)]

▲ *3.12 – And God said, Let there be light,*
and there was light. And God saw that the light was good.
And God separated the light from the darkness.

The Bible (Genesis 1:3,4)

SACRED MIRRORING

In an attempt to better understand the play of numbers present in the sacred books, it is necessary to redirect our attention to the mysterious primeval power-totality contained in a single point (One) that we also represent with a circle. To be able to find out more about itself, to fully experience its own potential, it has started the process we call *Genesis* or *Creation*.

We could look to Creation as to an eternal metamorphosis of One that witnesses the properties of its own perpetual isness. The *vesica pisces* is manifested on what, after the story told in *Genesis,* is called the *first day* of this immeasurable adventure (Fig. 3.12). As seen in chapter I, *One is Many,* the appearance of the *vesica pisces* was exceptionally significant because it exposed duality as the prime nature of Creation. Thus polarity, like male-female or active-passive, never ceases to exist.

The *vesica pisces* is a particular form of unity structured in a way that creates the illusion of separation. The perception of separation actually originates from the context in which the observation is made, for separation is only an impression based on a restricted view. Even opposites have something in common that links them and soothes their tensions.

Analysing the *tetraktys* in the book *All is Number*, we have seen that to the ancient Greeks, the existence of Two also implied the existence of the third factor. With Two, the third factor closes the triangle thus forming a common field that binds them all into a stable unity. Every group made of Two is a disguised *Holy Trinity* – since there is no Two without the presence of the third factor, acting like the Holy Spirit between them.

Harmony, symmetry and the dual nature of Creation *(as above, so below)* is captured in the geometry of the figure consisting of two opposite-facing triangles, within the *vesica pisces,* that share the same base (Fig.3.13). They segregate properties, virtues, elements and affairs, by positioning them into either of the two domains they create. Those two triangles represent unified fields defined by the initial point O, its replica O_1, and the pole M (in the upward-pointing triangle) and M_1 (in the downward-pointing triangle).

Every point in these two fields has its counterpoint in the opposite triangle. For example, point R of the OO_1M triangle has its reflection, R_1, in the opposite field of the triangle OO_1M_1, illustrating that nothing is single. Following this example, we could represent the primal creative principle with a simple yet eloquent glyph: ЯR. According to *The Knowledge Book,* this is the emblem of the *Mechanism of Lords*[(III-12)]. It symbolises the origin of *natural energy* – a *seed,* a *soul,* of all living Creation. Its form nicely indicates the dual nature of Creation and the power that keeps opposite forces in a strong symbiosis. That power is merely the ingenuity of the Creator who knows how to maintain His own order and balance.

Consciousnesses who can enter the Influence Field of every Word Uttered will never be the Human Being the Morrows Expect.

Vedia Bülent (Önsü) Çorak – (Light)

Formula of Light is a mathematical method which shows the way in which the sound energy, after exciting the ear drum, continues to spread towards the brain in the form of nerve impulses of an electromagnetic nature. It is an anthropomorphous formula of transformation of the sound into electromagnetic energy. The physical measures of that transformation of sounds into the electromagnetic spectrum are values we called the light states of sounds. Expressed as frequencies, which as a cosmic determination of light we perceive in form of colours, light states of sounds are the most important ring in the chain of correspondence between decimal numbers, coloured expressions, electromagnetic spectra and meanings.

Spasoje Vlajić

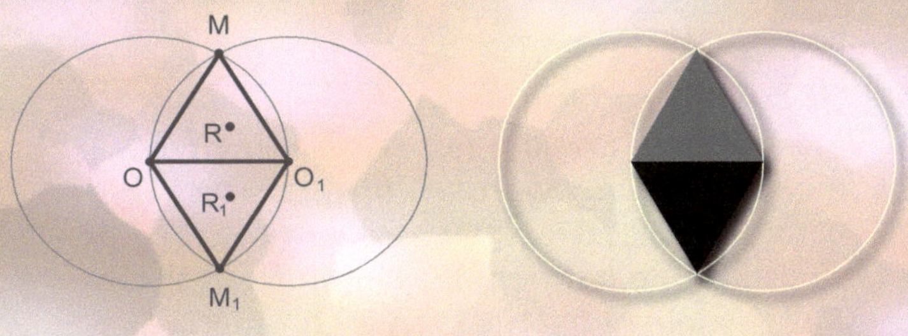
M
R
O
O1
R1
M1

▲ *3.13 – Nothing is single, since symmetry is a prime principle of Creation*

▼ *3.14 – The play of triangles and Kosh snowflake*

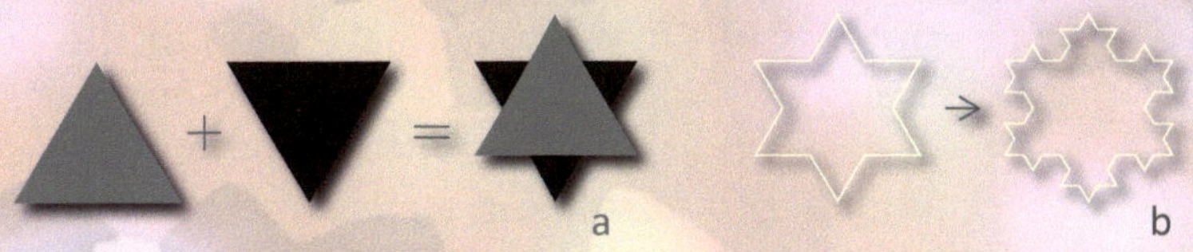
a
b

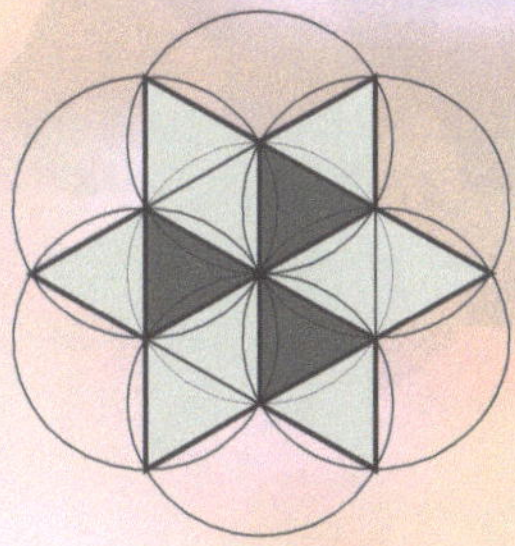

▲ *3.15 – How many triangles hide in this flower?*

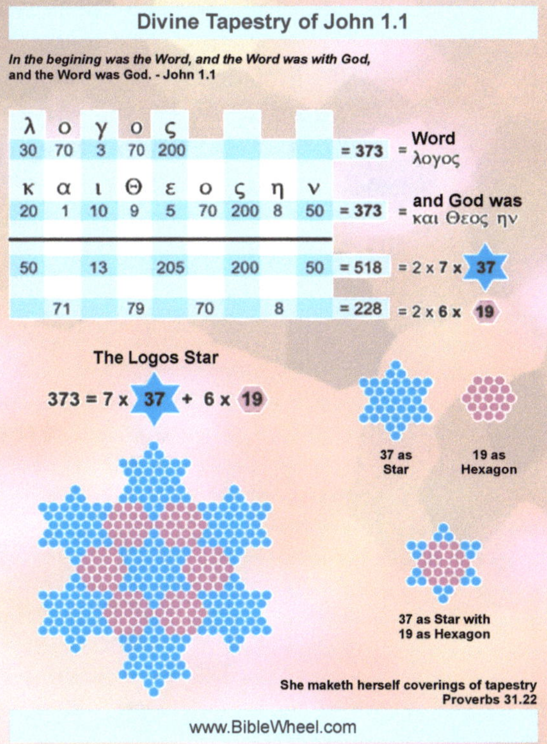
Divine Tapestry of John 1.1
In the begining was the Word, and the Word was with God, and the Word was God. - John 1.1
λ ο γ ο ς
30 70 3 70 200 = 373 = Word λογος
κ α ι Θ ε ο ς η ν
20 1 10 9 5 70 200 8 50 = 373 = and God was και Θεος ην
50 13 205 200 50 = 518 = 2 x 7 x 37
71 79 70 8 = 228 = 2 x 6 x 19
The Logos Star
373 = 7 x 37 + 6 x 19
37 as Star
19 as Hexagon
37 as Star with 19 as Hexagon
She maketh herself coverings of tapestry
Proverbs 31.22
www.BibleWheel.com

▲ *3.16 – Analysis of the Biblical sentence (John 1:1), using isopsephia, and design by* ***Richard Amiel McGough***

In the beginning was the Word,
and the Word was with God,
and the Word was God.

Looking again at this statement from *The Bible* (John 1:1), it is possible to notice that the numerical expression 1:1, under which it is announced, indicates reflection and symmetry as if discreetly pointing out their importance in the process of Creation. The *vesica pisces* epitomises these principles and is a primary transformational pattern based on self-mirroring.

So highly esteemed as to equal God, how significant is the Word for the beginning of Creation?

DIVINE SNOWING

If we start from the first two triangles of Creation formed within the *vesica pisces*, and shift them to symmetrically overlap one another, we will produce the recognisable shape of a regular hexagram (Fig. 3.14a). Coordinates of this figure were determined on the *sixth day of Creation* when the so-called *first pattern of Genesis* was created (Fig. 3.15). The final shape (b) shown in the same figure (Fig.3.14), comes from adding twelve smaller triangles to the hexagram (a), following the fractal principle of the *Kosh snowflake*.

The shape (b) featured in the figure 3.14 is, at the same time, an exact contour of the geometrical form of the number 373 when represented as a *figurate number*. Interestingly, the *Divine Tapestry of John* (Fig. 3.16), produced by the American **Richard Amiel McGough**[III-13], shows that particular regular complex star to be a geometrical image of the number 373 obtained by the *isopsephia*[III-14] as the numerical value of the Greek word *Logos* (meaning *Word*) (Fig 3.19).

Focusing for a moment on the *star figurate numbers,* it is possible to notice many of their relevances to the process of Creation. We have seen in the book *All is Number,* how the number Thirteen is an unchanging symbol of the Lord and the numerical value of the Hebrew words: *unity* and *love.* The number Seven accompanies the number Thirteen like its busy executive agent in the most sacred creational processes, and as its supreme structure establisher. The harmonious closeness of these two numbers is evident from the number Seven comfortably inhabiting the hexagonal area within the star shape of the number Thirteen (Fig. 3.18).

The first echo of the pair number 7/13 is the pair 19/37 which forms the same kind of *star figurate number* (Fig. 3.16). Coincidently, the numbers 19 and 37 are numerical representations of the Hebrew word *heart* according to *gematria,* counted in both *sequential value* (19) and *numerical value* (37). Also, an alphanumerical analysis of the Greek word *Gaia* or *Gaea,* meaning *Earth,* and the Arabic word *Wahid,* meaning *One,* results in the number 19.

The next more complex relative within the family of *star figurate numbers* is the pair 37/73, where 73 is a star with 37 as a hexagon within it. In his book, *The Bible Wheel,* **Richard Amiel McGough** reveals that the sum of the seven Hebrew words, with 28 letters all together, of the opening verse of *The Bible* (Genesis 1:1 – *In the beginning God created the Heavens and the Earth)* has *gematric* value 2701, which equals 37x73. In addition, the Hebrew word *wisdom* has *gematric* value of 73.

From this insight into the *star figurate numbers* (13, 37, 73), and their hexagonal central companions (7, 19, 37), it is possible to see how some of them are numerical representatives of the words like *One, love, Earth, wisdom* and how the first Biblical verse of *Genesis* is ciphered through the *star numbers* 37 and 73.

Further on, we can notice that the *star figurate number* 373 maintains a strong connection with the *star number* 13 on many levels. Not only does the number 373 echo the star shape of the number Thirteen, but the number 169 (the central hexagon of the 373-star) is the square of Thirteen (13^2=169). Also, in the star configuration of the number 373 there are six hexagons (red) and seven hexagrams (blue), making it in total thirteen clearly evident figures (Fig. 3.16). Interestingly, the six hexagrams on the periphery numerically add up to the *master number* 222 (37x6=222), while the sum of the six hexagons in the central part of this complex star is 114 (6x19=114), which incidentally is the number of chapters in *The Quran.*

The word *Word (Logos,* in Greek) has an intriguing relation to the word *mishlag (of snow,* in Hebrew). Alphanumerical analysis reveals that these words have the same numerical value of 373[III-14]. This means they both take the geometry of a complex snowflake when represented as a 373-*star figurate number* (3.19).

▲ *3.17 – Number 19 structured through 7*

▶*3.18 – The essence-energy of the Mighty Energy Focal Point, in the Main Existential Dimension of the Gürz crystal, is expressed through the number 13*[III-15]

Since
in God's
workshop there
are no coincidences,
this example illustrates a
deep interconnectedness within His
Creation.

In chapter I, *One is Many,* we could follow the *Genesis* of geometrical forms and the way they are encoded in the *flower of life* figure.

If we compare the geometries of the *373-Logos star* and the *flower of life* figure, by now we should not be too surprised to discover that they are a perfect match, since both are elemental tools of Creation (Fig. 3.19).

One is the way of form/matter/technology entrusted to geometry and the other is the way of sound entrusted to the *Word*. As two faces belonging to the same coin, the potential of these two deeply harmonious complementary patterns (Fig. 3.20), serves the same purpose, that of Creation. The *flower of life* is a geometrical archetype of the form, while the *Word/sound* animates forms defined by geometry (breathing life into the form).

Words are propagated by sound. Whether audible or silent, sound does to words what wind does to pollen when it spreads the essence of a flower into distant places. If, instead of entering a discordant environment, *Word* manages to reach or create a vibrationally compatible ground, that word empowers itself and fulfils its own purpose – like pollen that secures the future of the flower by pollinating it.

Looking at this wonderful symbiosis of the *373-Logos star* and the *flower of life,* we can notice the repetition of certain geometrical forms associated with centred *hexagonal* and *star figurate numbers.*

3.19 –
▲ *According to isopsephia, the alphanumerical value of the Greek word LOGOS (meaning WORD) is 373 and the divine snowflake (above) is a geometrical form of that figurate number.*

▼ *The flower of life is a figure based on 19 equal whole spheres/circles.*

... Love, therefore, is the fulfilment of the law.

The Bible
(Romans 13:10)

▲ 3.20 – The *flower of life* is an ideal template for the star figurate number 373, which is alphanumerical value of the word LOGOS (WORD, in Greek)

Philosophy is written in this grand book – I mean the universe – which stands continually open to our gaze, but it cannot be understood unless one first learns to comprehend the language and interpret the characters in which it is written. It is written in the language of mathematics, and its characters are triangles, circles, and other geometrical figures, without which it is humanly impossible to understand a single word of it.

Galileo Galilei[III-16]

One of the greatest instruments for practical development, lying in the hands of small and great, is the instrument of SPEECH. He who guards his words, and who only speaks with altruistic purpose, in order to carry the energy of Love through the medium of the tongue, is one who is mastering rapidly the initial steps to be taken in preparation for initiation.

Speech is the most occult manifestation in existence; IT IS THE MEANS OF CREATION and the vehicle of force. In the reservation of words, esoterically understood – lies the conservation of force; in the utilisation of words, justly chosen and spoken – lies the distribution of the love force of the solar system, that force which preserves, strengthens, and stimulates.

Djwhal Khul[III-17]

The *figurate numbers* dwelling in these patterns are 6, 7, 13, 19 and 37, and they have been repeatedly emphasised through sacred scriptures and other spiritual traditions. The number Three is also there to connect every three points, and to turn the whole design into a performance of triangles (Fig. 3.21).

The number Seven appears far too frequently in Biblical texts to be ignored, while *The Knowledge Book* reveals it to be the number behind the unchanging essence of the atomic structure of the *centrifugal universe*[III-18].

The number 19, the number of whole spheres/circles on which the *flower of life* figure is born, prevails in *The Quran* while most recent discoveries indicate its deep connection with the Periodic table of the elements.

From further observation of the *flower of life*, and the *373-Logos star,* we can notice that one pattern is made of curves (the *flower of life*) while the other is composed of straight lines (the 373-*Logos star*). Their compatibility illustrates an immaculate balance of the opposite principles.

LIGHT ORIGIN OF LETTERS

The cosmos seen from inside is light, and seen from outside is thought. The human head seen from inside is thought, and seen from outside is light…

You see, light and thought belong together. Light and thought are the same thing, seen from different sides.

Rudolf Steiner
(Colour)

*Who in all his work sees God,
he in truth goes unto God.*

Krishna[(III-20)]
(Bhagavad-Gita)

We have observed the significance of geometry and the *Word* in the process of Creation as well as the importance of light in transporting information and delivering meaning. Nevertheless, light seems to be an even more interesting component of life. Recent studies of the alphabet indicate the light-origin of letters and their connection to DNA. Analyses of the Sanskrit, Hebrew, Greek and Arabic alphabets suggest that letters might be derived as fragments of the *golden spiral,* captured at certain angles, while moving along a torus.

The light-origin of some alphabets, implying mathematical principles behind the shape of letters, is a new yet acceptable premise. If fully explored and recognised, it could change the direction of our thinking with regards to the principal source of knowledge. Thus the role of light and geometry in the evolution of consciousness would also become more evident.

Our brain and each of our cells provide a vehicle for the Totality of Consciousness (through Light) to function in its micro format. Light is the nourishment not only for our tangible physical body but for our spiritual self as well. By charging our light batteries, the Life-Power is delivered to us. Light is also our truest guide towards the ultimate fulfilment of our divine purpose. Through the light that permeates our being, eternity has always lived in us.

◀ *3.21 – The 373-Logos star decomposed into triangles*

▲ *3.22 – The way towards form – information/energy flow[(III-21)]*

Shape carries information and is the result of the relationships of its own dimensions, rather than their value. Thus the only way to preserve shape is to maintain the relationships of its dimensions (ratio). To Daniel Winter – ratio is sacred, scale is profane.

There is such a Photo-synthesis within the Dark that each Colour melts within it and thus, creates that Black Medium. This is a hot Medium. Darkness is the richest Medium of the Universe and the Total. For this reason, all the Energies have assembled in that intense Black.

The Knowledge Book (F54, p 949, par 1)

Waves	Wave length
	1000 Mm
3.23 – The electromagnetic radiation spectrum	10 Mm
	1 Mm
	100 km
	10 km
Radio	1 km
	100 m
	10 m
	1 m
	100 mm
Microwaves	10 mm
	1 mm
	100 m
Infrared	10 m
	1 m
Visible Light	
Ultraviolet	100 nm
	10 nm
X-Rays	1 nm
	100 pm
	10 pm
	1 pm
Gamma	100 fm
	10 fm
	1 fm

Doubt leading to goodness moves on a circle and circling along it reaches the starting point. Doubt leading to malevolence moves in a strait line, without looking back and turning, and never meets the starting point.

Nikolai Velimirovic[III-22]

The strait Line corresponds to the Even Numbers because it terminates at Two Points, and the Circular to the Odd because it is composed of a single Line without Terminus.

Theon of Smyrna[III-23]

▶ *3.24 – Shape is a finite construct made up of lines while spirals appear as a route to its regular movement/harmonic growth on an infinite course.*

Apart from the sphere, archetypal shapes known as the Platonic solids are all composed of strait lines.

In the book *Golden proportion,* it was possible to see how the most appreciated harmonies and proportions in art, nature, and even our inner world, are achieved by the *golden proportion* which is a divine formula for beauty and self-regulated order on all levels of Creation – from fractal nesting of atomic particles to the planetary world. Chapter on *Spirals* (the book *Cosmic Diagrams*) revealed how the *golden proportion* smoothly acts through the *golden spiral,* maintaining its immaculate dynamism on the journey between infinities. The perfect everlasting harmonies of beyondness, introduced through the *golden proportion,* we sense in beauty and love from which our divine longing is triggered.

Beauty and love are seeds of eternity.

Love is an aspect of light. Love is a vibration transmitted by the divine waves to sustain matter, after having created it formerly.

We reach both beauty and love through the evolution of our consciousness, in proportion to the opening of our essence.

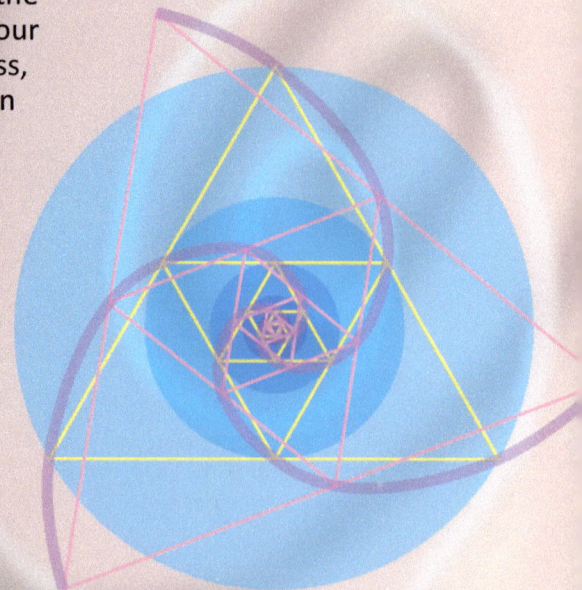

Some modern scientists have started to observe love in a wider than usual context. Through his ether-wave theory **Daniel Winter**, for example, explains gravity as the result of a loving attraction of interacting waves. Not only does their harmonic compression, according to him, create gravity (implosion); it also creates matter.

The potential power of our thoughts was documented in the research and findings of the Russian **Nikolay Kozyrev** (1908-1983) who studied *scalar waves* (calling them *torsion waves)*. In the 1950's he scientifically proved that our thoughts and feelings produce *torsion waves* which expand far beyond our body. They travel in a field-like manner at a speed that can be faster than the speed of light. Carried by these waves, each of our thoughts heads towards its cosmic destination to realise its own purpose.

Scalar waves are a component of *electromagnetic waves* that always existed as energy, though long hidden from scientists. In his 1899 experiments, the Serb **Nikola Tesla** demonstrated their presence thus discovering a form of energy independent of gravity. Due to their infinite energy, *Tesla's waves* did not lose their intensity at long distances even after he projected them through the Earth.

Apart from being capable of passing through solid objects, these unusual waves are able to change the rate time flows and affect the mass of an object, as well as our thoughts and mind.

Scalar waves can be generated magnetically, electronically, optically or physically by the simple actions of spinning, shaking, heating, cooling, vibrating, or relocating an item, or by the very geometry of some shapes like a pyramid. Every physical object makes its own energy imprint in the fabric of its surroundings. After an object is moved, its remaining scalar wave particles hold the memory of it at the location it has left.

That is the way the ether keeps a record of all happenings, from the tiniest movements to complex events. Like a new colour, every single wave adds its own value to the tapestry of life. Having infinite energy, *scalar waves* are perfect keepers and carriers of information.

Experiments have revealed that *scalar waves,* created either through scalar wave technology, human thoughts, or some other means, can also be imprinted on water thereby altering its structure. If recorded, then any alteration, in response to an influence, can be called memory. Since water preserves its own new configuration generated by *scalar* waves, this implies that water has ways to remember. If water has a mechanism that hosts memory, then each matter, through its cellular awareness, could also remember according to its own evolutionary level.

▲ *3.25 – Electromagnetic waves are a vehicle for the transportation of electromagnetic energy (radiation). Electrical and magnetic components of this force are propagated through two fields that are orthogonal to each other: electrostatic energy spreads through the horizontal plane while magnetic energy spreads through the vertical plane.*

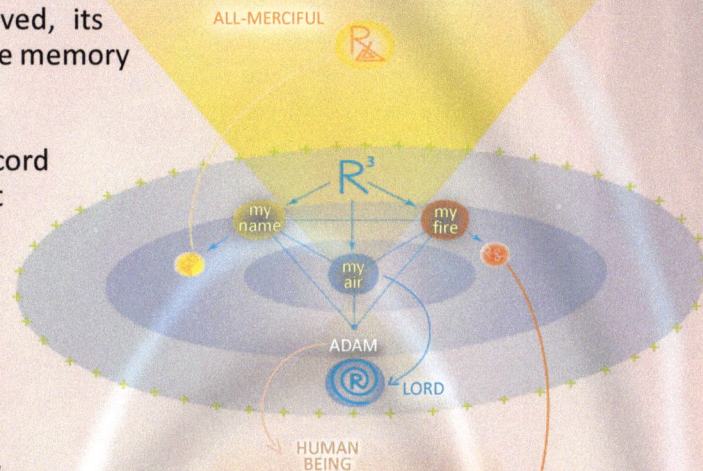

ALL-MERCIFUL

R³

my name
my fire
my air

ADAM

LORD

HUMAN BEING

Pre-Eminent Power (R¹), from its own essence, has brought into existence three energy totalities in the Second Universe (My Name, My Air and My Fire) which jointly, in a laboratory work, created ADAM then EVE.

ALL-DOMINATING

Upon the natural Gürz formation, these three energy totalities emerged as administrative powers of the Gürz crystal:

- *ALL-MERCIFUL – (My Name)*
- *LORD – (My Air)*
- *ALL-DOMINATING – (My Fire)*

The symbol of these three administrative powers is R³; thus the Pre-Eminent Power, who has created them, is also called R⁹(III-24)

In space, there is a static entelechy that makes everything move and thought is its major attribute. The energy of one thought can determine the movement of the cosmos.

Nikola Tesla

Beauty and scent of roses can be used as a medicine, and Light as a food.

Nikola Tesla

Whenever Beauty looks, Love is also there.

Mevlana Celaleddin-i Rumi

1919 Ω 1991

▼ *3.26 – While illustrating that geometry is inherent in sound, as its vibrational skeleton, the CymaGlyph of the vowel O reveals the perfect seal pattern which we have seen behind the energy unification style of the Light-Universes. O is also an aspect of the Consciousness Totality. In this Totality, called ALLAH, there are numberless Totalities of TRUTH where O is an Order and a System that supervises its own Dimension – the Dimension of Allah (O). From that dimension, Consciousness Totality is reflected onto the Ocean of Consciousness and from there onto the Ocean of Thoughts*[III-26]*. Thus, all entities gain CONSCIOUSNESS parallel to the purity, maturity and power of their THOUGHTS. (CymaGlyph by John Reid, the perfect seal emphasised by Milena)*

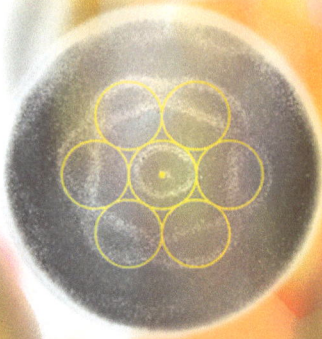

Awareness units are the invisible building blocks of Creation in which all that carries energy is in touch through the language of its own vibrational domain. Even solid matter objects, when they like us, have their way of attracting our attention to convey to us their wish to be bought. However, once in our possession, by their cellular awareness they can choose to be destroyed if they find our energy inadequate to their evolutionary needs[III-25]. Our kitchen table may well remember the forest where it once lived as a tree. Without the use of a mobile phone, it can exchange information with its then neighbouring tree, that might reside on the other side of the globe shaped as a cupboard. Objects hold memory and communicate inside their own magnetic dimensions.

Science tells us that physical objects radiate or absorb *scalar waves*. At the level of these waves, life is an unceasing flux of everything influencing everything and doing it everywhere. Continuous emanations of our being influence our environment while, at the same time, the environment shapes our energy field. Within the one single web of life we are all together, weaving our reality with even the minutest of thoughts. With every passing moment we sculpt ourselves. If we are fully aware of it, then it is a conscious act. In a give-take process, meaning defines itself.

What are shapes telling us? Truly, that the consciousness operating behind their energy chooses shapes to explore its own potentials through them. Divine purpose is shaping the energy, thus shapes are sacred. They capture the Creator's intentions and deliver them, epitomising His imagination. Shapes are custodians of viable proportions, therefore of relations, therefore of the formulae for harmonious coexistence and for accomplishing an order. As creative parameters, ratios establish rules and allow shapes to best serve in the direction of their purpose. Size, or scale, is of secondary importance in God's workshop.

In the universe made of particle-wave and wave-particle vibrations, shapes are also the result of wave interference. The cymatics' experiments showed that sand moved from the areas of prominent vibrations to those where it could stay motionless (Fig. 3.26; 2.1, 2.2). Matter appears at the places where the waves cancel each other's influence, or at least slow down their vibrational rate. Form is thus a diagram of forces.

At this point we will return to a particular aspect of the scientific efforts that coloured the research of **Nikola Tesla**, and of **Spasoje Vlajić** who was inspired by him.

Apart from having the mind of a genius, being fluent in seven languages and possessing challenging ideas, **Tesla** never lost his simplicity, modesty and his human and noble attitudes towards life, nature and the Spirit. **Tesla**'s dream was for man to conquer his own mind, and by his own will, based on good intentions, emerge as a sovereign being. He believed humans on planet Earth would one day co-create with nature and cosmic forces and so genuinely align with the Creator. **Spasoje Vlajić** spent years of research to realise **Tesla**'s vision. For both of these men of scientific mind, the way to their dream was the way of beauty and love.

Beauty is a result of harmony and order. Order structures elements in a most economical way, be they in our thoughts, emotions or in space. The perception of chaos requires more energy than the perception of beauty. Disorder exhausts us since it is puzzling and we do not know its rules. To deal with it in a constructive manner, a visionary approach and also considerable mental, emotional and often physical efforts are needed. Those unfortunately are not always available. However, being synonymous with uncertainty, chaos is also a fertile soil which can provide numerous directions for moving forward. It is unstable in its nature and can be seen as a transition state that lives between two orders. Chaos waits for powerful forces of order to transform it.

On the other hand, beauty, as a result of order, symmetry and harmony, requires less energy from us. It is a self-sustainable structure based on the coherent relationship of its elements. Beauty is a supreme quality of our being hence when we encounter it outside us, we are reminded of the truth of our own essence. Each time we experience beauty, we are a step closer to God and our true self.

Beauty is a form of love spread through a particular vocabulary that excites our divine core. It is an expression of a consciousness that transcends disorder and finds refuge in order and harmony from where it emanates its truth. Our senses enable us to experience beauty. They send information to our soul, for beauty to be savoured as its sublime food. Beauty is a golden thread, a psycho-physical quality that transcends logic and time.

Beauty attracts, for it is so balanced that the life-force joyfully, effortlessly and continuously flows through it. That charge is freely on offer to the consumer. Beauty invites us beyond the ephemeral, to the sacred area of its origin. Beauty of any kind is a sample of eternity.

After the formation of the Second Universe, the Atlanta Dimension initiated the "big bang" project.

The first energy ball, closest to the Second Universe, that cooled down was Earth. From here, both the programme of the Atomic Whole formation (Gürz (crystal) and the soul seed project have started. Through the laboratory work on our planet, Adam-kind, brought into existence in the Second Universe and engrafted with the genes from the Atlanta dimension, created Human-kind[III-28].

big bang

CREATOR (R*)

Second universe

Supreme MATU (ALLAH)

ALMIGHTY

earth

2 LIGHT

8

FIRE

1 SOUND

ATLANTA dimension

Let the beauty we love Be what we do.

Mevlana Celaleddin-i Rumi

The findings of **Dr Masaru Emoto** reveal beauty to be inherent in positive thoughts and intentions, words and some works of music. Water demonstrates that our thoughts and feelings affect it according to the principle of symmetry: what we hold inside appears outside of us. Water crystals mirror our inner world exposing its hidden geometrical aspect. We are obviously more than just a visible physical body which we tend to squeeze ourselves into. We stretch to infinity with every breath, thought, word and smile we make. Emanations of our being touch and affect everything, whether it is an animate or inanimate object, since all are energy beings anyway. What a responsibility this awareness brings to us!

From **Dr Emoto**'s experiments we have the chance to learn about the importance of our commitment to affirmative attitudes. They will produce an exquisite quality in the water molecules of our body so that the life-force will gracefully enliven our body and mind. We can all become a walking display of ceaseless twinkling of light when purified enough to think good only and when we begin to act like fathomless fountains of *respect, love* and *gratitude*. We will arrive to this stage subsequent to us living through all we need to, in order to realise that for the most meaningful way of living the full control of our thoughts, words and actions is a must. When all other modes of existence become inadequate, inevitably will we activate such a level of self.

Disciplining our minds and personalities means disciplining our biological forms. Such a multilevelled alignment results in both harmony and beauty that spread out from within us. The meeting of cellular and cerebral awareness at the same coordinate also signifies the c o m p l e t i o n of a huge evolutionary step.

Hence our essence claims its power from the *spiritual dimension* while new universal avenues open wide before us to challenge our ever-expanding consciousness.

Beauty comes from opening ourselves to the Creator's Love. The genuine faith in that love manifests itself through a total acceptance of God's Will. With an unconditional surrendering to God's Will, comes a lightness of being as a particular form of beauty. Our alignment with the divine flow becomes stronger as we purify and calm our body and mind thus enabling the universal forces of Creation to express themselves through us.

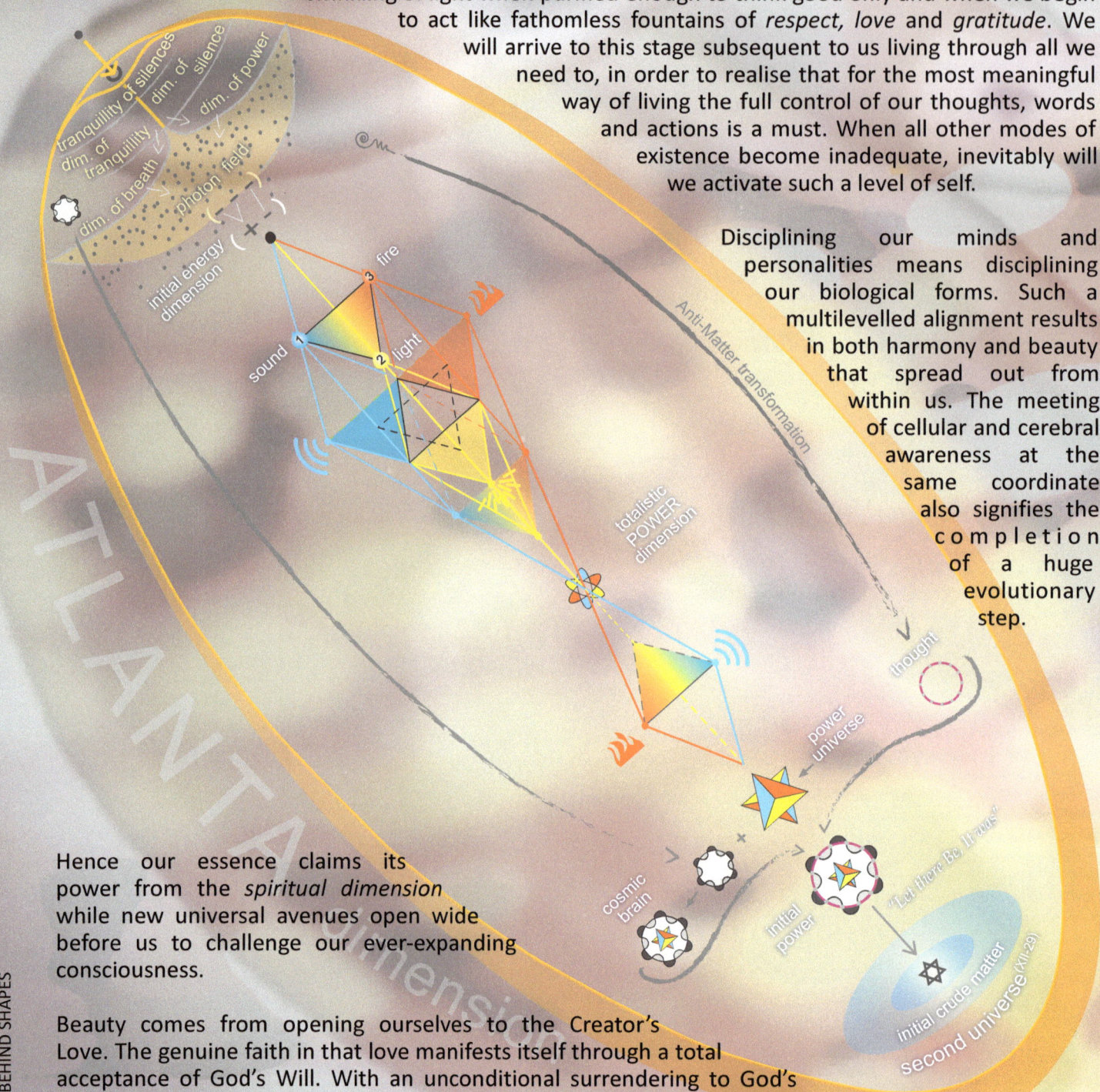

Our brain is perfectly attuned to receive both earthly and cosmic signals. It is an abode for our thoughts in which the registration of impulses from various dimensions of influence and their subsequent transformation into meanings pertinent to our level of consciousness take place. Thoughts connect us with the primal life source. The moment our brain ceases to work, we close one chapter in our book of incarnations and head on towards celestial station to wait for the opening of another chapter necessary for our further evolvement.

The ability to utter words is our gift from God. Words are effective carriers of light and love. Words are born from thoughts hence thoughts are their light seeds. Cosmic currents sent to our planet, continuously deliver the light/information needed for our evolution. These special celestial influences enlarge our evolutionary capacity and facilitate our faster transformation into a greater light and greater love. Thus, we offer our ever more sparkling feedback to Creation. God's love has always been invigorating us in proportion to our ability to receive and process divine waves.

Humans are designed as perfect energy devices that receive, transmute and transmit energy. By interpreting the meanings of all that we encounter, on the basis of free will, we can choose to constantly beautify and enlighten ourselves. That is the biggest service to the Creator and to Creation that we can perform. Human beings are capable of generating good will and love, and our evolution at this stage is directly dependant on this God-given power. Guarding the inner light by consciously upholding the frequencies of love is the work of an awakened being. To cultivate ourselves in that direction is the noblest of tasks in existence.

In every breath we take, the Creator lovingly watches us. He knows each of our thoughts and feelings. What are we to do with the light of love He has made so available to us? For a start, let us think only those thoughts the realisation of which we would gladly live.

He is with you wherever you may be. GOD is Seer of everything you do.

The Quran (57:4)

FORCE OF MEANING CONNECTS US WITH THE HEAVENS

Whatever we think or say will eventually attract its physical counterpart. As **Spasoje Vlajić** explains, a meeting of mental and physical images on the same coordinate is the result of the interdimensional functioning of the force of meaning. The common meaning is the one that attracts and gathers similar energies. When a critical point in amassing similar energies is achieved, by the law of turning quantity into quality, manifestation takes place. It is therefore immensely important to take responsibility for our own thoughts and experiences. The development of a skill to control our thoughts, equally strengthens our ability to manage what we create. Confidence born this way turns us into masters of life.

On the road to that mastery, the supremacy of the Word is yet to be learnt. Only now do we seem to be ready to fully grasp the real meaning behind the two-thousand- year old message, that *John* in *The Bible* passed to humanity intending to point our attention to the sacred power of the Word.

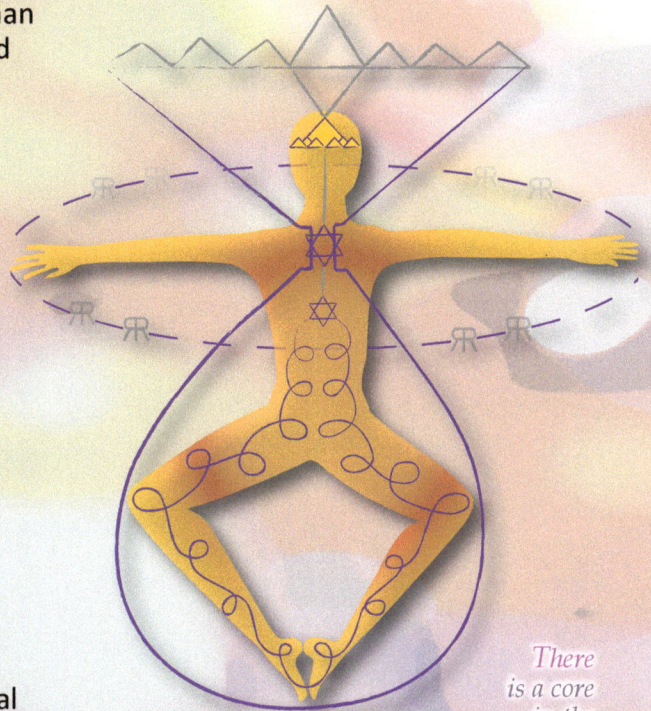

There is a core in the cosmos that gives all our power to us, all inspirations... When I want to give it a material attribute, then I think it is Light, and when I try to understand it spiritually, then it is beauty and compassion.

Nikola Tesla

What one thinks, that he become – this is the mystery of eternity.

Gautama Buddha(III-30)

As a creational instrument of the Spirit, the *Word* is governed by the laws of the Spirit. It acquires its greatest power only when accompanied by frequencies of love, harmony and peace. Human beings of the lower frequencies, therefore, cannot fully use its creative potential. **Vlajić** revealed that the *alpha* state (8-13Hz) of brain function, at around 10Hz, is the most suitable one for the transformation of our mental pictures and words into tangible physical events of corresponding meaning. *Alpha* brain frequencies are in the same range as the Earth's resonant frequency known as the *Schumann resonance*[(III-31)]. This indicates the necessity for us to adjust our frequency to that of the higher sphere of being, in order for our thoughts and words to materialise. Harmony with Mother Earth is thus an imperative. If we achieve it, as a result of constructive congruence of micro and macro information fields, manifestation occurs.

It seems that the *force of meaning* connects us with the heavens by manifesting our thoughts through an interaction of the physical with the so-called metaphysical. Inquisitiveness in this area has laid a foundation for a new science. It is the physics and technology of consciousness and it is part of other sciences that are slowly embracing higher spiritual values as grounds for their research. Love, beauty, betterment for all, wholeness and compassion, are their prime inspirations. The work of **Tesla** and **Vlajić** is entirely based on these ideals.

FLAP YOUR WINGS

Uttered words are a communication tool carried by energy of their source, backed by the force of meaning. The sacred books inform us about the creative power of the *Word*, since God has started the entire process of Creation by a single word. The *Word* conceived by the Creator is a depository of supreme vibrations that we recognise as unconditional love, unity, beauty, acceptance and kindness, but we are yet to learn how to provide these through our words.

Words dwelling in our mind colour our thoughts. Our personal thought-rainbows are in a constant search for compatible colour patterns outside us. Once these are found, we are invigorated, witnessing the principles of resonance and symmetry that support our identity.

God really loves and believes in us greatly, since He has given us access to such power as words have. Though we spell them all our life, are we actually aware that each one of them can hugely enrich life with love and beauty, and might ultimately be capable of creating a universe? The *flower of life* is a geometrical blueprint of Creation. Its potential to define form is infinite. Word/Sound is its perfect complement, or its particular synonymous. That which can fully operate these prime creational tools is the God-Self only.

My intention is not to make an airplane or a rocket, but to help human beings recover awareness of their own wings.

Nikola Tesla[(III-32)]

You will not enter paradise, until you believe. And you will not believe, until you love one another.

Mohammed Mustafa
(Prophet)

We have had the potential of the God-Self from the moment of our first conception. Our long-lasting sleep is being interrupted by the energy of time that is calling us from beyond. Our awakening is divinely scheduled. Each of our cells knows it. They already work diligently, upgrading our physical vehicle and preparing it to spread its wings and fly. The heavens are nearer than ever. They have always been touching the Earth, but now they have opened their depths so that the two vastnesses can embrace. The veil is being removed. Once we start believing in this, we will be able to fully spread our wings and fly into the unknown. As long as our gyroscope is in our heart, wherever we fly to – we will fly home. The Creator is in everything. His love is everywhere. Mesmerised by that newly discovered ability, we might never stop flying.

Let us exercise our wings in silence and gratitude, and start strengthening them. If the wings do not seem to be there yet, may we think them into being. Let us awake our God within and let Him do the magic. Each and every moment, may we spell our future with care and love. The Being of space is not only surrounding us and watching us, but is listening to us as well. It overhears our thoughts and absorbs our verbal expressions, using their geometrical templates to mould them into tangible forms.

There is an exquisite elegance in numbers and geometry. It is the elegance of God that resides throughout Creation – in our cells as in our love – His love. The beautiful symmetry and power of this ONE LOVE hold us all together.

Every shape is a custodian of that truth.

▲ 3.27 – An eternal LOVE affair is an unending embrace.
In the etheric substance of God,
WE ARE ALL ONE

All of mankind are children,
except for those
who are drunk with God.
No-one is mature
who is not free of self-will.

Mevlana Celaleddin-i Rumi

ONE IS MANY

I-1 Images in the following illustrations are based on the corresponding ones from the book *The ANCIENT SECRETS of the FLOWER OF LIFE* by Drunvalo Malchizedek, with his kind permission: 1.2, 1.3, 1.9, 1.15a, 1.17, 1.19, 1.20, 1.23, 1.25, 1.31, 1.32, 1.33, 1.34 and 1.35.

I-2 St. Maximus the Confessor, (580-662), Constantinople-born theologian, one of the most prominent writers of the Greek Church. Some of his books are *Four Centuries of Love, Ambigua and Mystagogia*.

I-3 Flo Aeveia Magdalena is an author, medium, healer and teacher who founded *Soul Support Systems* and the *Heaven On Earth Global Community;* www.soulsupportsystems.org

I-4 Messages from The GROUP first came to Steve Rother in 1996. Translated into 11 languages so far, they have filled several books since (see the back cover). The monthly *Beacons of Light – Reminders from Home* have been translated into 21 languages and presented at the United Nations five times; www.lightworker.com

I-5 Daniel Winter, a writer and lecturer in the areas of electrical engineering, psychophysiology (the origin of languages), computer animation in multimedia and non-linear energy source technologies. Winter developed superior technology for measuring coherent emotions in the heart *(HeartTuner*, also called *BlissTuner)*. In his research and practical work he bridges the physical with the metaphysical; www.fractalfield.com

I-6 Yael and Doug Powell, *Messages from God;* www.circleoflight.net

I-7 Ibrahim F. Karim, PhD, Egyptian architect, the father of the new science of BioGeometry™. With Rawya Karim, MA, he founded the *BioGeometrical Systems Institute Company* in 1993 as a design centre for research and implementation of BioGeometry™. For more information about their work see chapter III, *MESSAGES BEHIND SHAPES;* www.biogeometry.com

I-8 Ronna Herman is an internationally known lecturer and author of eight books. The books and messages transmitted to her from Archangel Michael have been translated into most major languages and read around the world. You may contact her at: RonnaStar@earthlink.net, www.ronnastar.com

I-9 Frank van den Bovenkamp, *Heart Coherence team;* www.heartcoherence.com

I-10 Sheldan Nidle is a representative and lecturer for the *Galactic Federation of Light*. He founded the *Planetary Activation Organization (PAO)* in November 1997; www.paoweb.com

I-11 Seng Ts'an (520-606) was an ancient Chinese sage, the third patriarch of Zen Buddhism in China.

I-12 Lao Tzu (老子, 570BC-490BC – though many believe he never existed), was born in Ch'u (the present-day Henan Province in China). Lao Tzu literally means *Old Master*. He was a contemporary of Confucius in China as well as of Plato and Socrates in Greece, and Buddha in India. Lao Tzu is the founder of *Taoism*.

I-13 Shunryu Suzuki (dharma name: *Shogaku Shunryu*) (1904-1971) was a Japanese Zen master of Soto, who established Buddhism in America at the first Buddhist training monastery outside Asia. Quote from his book *Zen Mind, Beginner's Mind*.

I-14   According to Dr Rashad Khalifa's analysis of *The Quran*, *Bismillahir-Rahmanir-Rahim (In the Name of Allah, the Most Gracious, the Most Merciful)*, the opening verse of all but the ninth chapter of *The Quran,* appears 114 (19x6) times in *The Quran*. It consists of 19 Arabic letters and every word in *Bismillahir-Rahmanir-Rahim* throughout *The Quran* appears a number of times which is a multiple of 19.

I-15   Kryon – from the message channelled on 1st January 2003 through David Brown; kryon.org.za

I-16   Alphanumerical analysis, Richard Amiel McGough

I-17   On the significance of the number 19, see: Vedia Bülent (Önsü) Çorak, *The Knowledge Book,* Fascicule 6, pages 89-91

I-18   Johannes Kepler (1571-1630), German astronomer and mathematician from the time of the Holy Roman Empire. Influenced by Copernican teachings, he formulated three great laws of planetary motions, known as *Kepler's laws*, which describe the revolutions of the planets around the Sun. He worked as court mathematician to the Holy Roman Emperor Rudolf II. Wrote *Misterium Cosmographicum* (1596) and *Astronomia Nova* (1609). He proclaimed astrology a true science, and believed that certain harmonious configurations of planets influence human impulses. In 1724, the Russian empress Catharina the Great bought his manuscripts and deposited them in the observatory of Pulkovo, near St. Petersburg.

I-19   Josef Plečnik (1872-1957) was born in Ljubljana, in Austro-Hungary (present-day Slovenia). He studied architecture in Vienna with Otto Wagner, and worked with him until 1900. During the following ten years he continued to practice architecture in Vienna. In 1911 he moved to Prague where he taught at the college of arts and crafts. When the renovation of Prague Castle started, he was appointed chief architect. In 1921 Plečnik moved to Ljubljana to teach at Ljubljana University and remained there until the end of his life. His work was based on classical principles and folk-art traditions.

I-20   *Upanishads* are philosophical scriptures placed at the end of the Indian writings, *Vedas*. Dating from 1500BC-800BC, the *Vedas* represent the most ancient sacred texts of Hinduism. There are four *Vedas*: collections of hymns to the gods *(Rig Veda* – the oldest *Veda)*, chants and songs *(Sama Veda)*, incantations and magical spells *(Atharva Veda)* and instructions for rituals *(Yajur Veda)*. They were transmitted orally through generations of brahmans and eventually by 300BC were written in Sanskrit. Apart from *Upanishads*, each *Veda* has three more parts: *Mantras* (sacred formulae), *Brahmanas* (instructions for rituals) and *Aranyakas* ('forest texts'). *Katha Upanishad* is a story about the spiritual journey of a young boy. It is written in verse and describes his endeavours on the way to experiencing ultimate reality.

I-21   Pythagoras's theorem: *In any right angled triangle, the area of the square whose side is the hypotenuse* (the biggest side of a right-angled triangle) *is equal to the sum of the areas of the squares on the other two sides.* For this theorem the converse is also true: *for any three positive numbers a, b, and c such that* $a^2 + b^2 = c^2$, *there exists a triangle with sides a, b and c, and every such triangle has a right angle between the sides of lengths a and b.*

I-22   Socrates (Σωκράτης, 470BC-399BC) was an ancient Greek philosopher. He is considered the founder of western philosophy despite the fact that no work of Socrates has survived. We learn his doctrines from the writings of others, like those of his student Plato. Socrates was a lover of wisdom and promoter of the dialectic method of enquiry. He believed that focusing on personal development, as opposed to acquiring material wealth, was the best way to live. Accused of corrupting the youth of Athens, he was sentenced to death.

I-23   All attempts by the author to reveal the originator, and to contact the originator/guardian of this figure, have been to no avail. The same applies to the illustrations featured in figure 2.2. If you have information about them, please contact the author via the publishers in order to give proper acknowledgement.

MUSIC

II-1 Thoth, mythical immortal ruler and sage of ancient Egypt, was credited with the transfer of all knowledge and hieroglyphic writing to Egyptians. The ancient Greeks believed him to be the architect of the *Great Pyramid* and compared him with their own God Hermes, adding the attribute *Trismegistus (Trice-great)* to his name to make a distinction. The books assigned to the divine messenger Thoth are known as *Hermetica*, and are Africa's contribution to the treasure of ancient wisdom – the same as *Upanishads*, *Tao Te Ching* and *Dhammapada* are contributions from the Far East.

II-2 Mevlana Celaleddin-i Rumi (1207-1273) worldwide celebrated poet and Sufi mystic. Just like Zoroaster, he was born in the Persian city of Balkh (present-day North Afghanistan). A 3000-year-history makes Balkh one of the oldest cities in the world. Many cultures left their mark on it: Buddhists, Greeks with Alexander the Great, Arabs, and Mongols with Genghis Khan. Escaping from the Mongols in 1225, Rumi's father settled with his family in the city of Konya in Anatolia (Turkey), then part of the Turkish Seljuk Empire. Rumi was the founder of the Mevlevi Sufi order, a mystical brotherhood of Islam. His most famous work is a poetical interpretation of themes from *The Quran*, in the Pahlavi language, known as the *Mesnevi*.

II-3 Gottfried Wilhelm Leibniz (also *Leibnitz* or *von Leibniz)* (1646-1716) was a German polymath from the Luzice Serb minority. His philosophy, like those of Rene Descartes *(Cognito ergo sum)* and Baruch de Spinoza, was rationalism based on the belief that in theory all knowledge could be acquired through the use of reason. Educated in law and philosophy, with a distinctive optimism, and a strong inclination towards logic and analysis, Leibniz played an important role in the politics and diplomacy of his time. He also made noted contributions to technology, physics and mathematics, and pioneered notions in the fields of quantum mechanics, relativity, fractals, information science, geology and psychology. He also wrote on law, ethics, politics, philology, theology and history.

II-4 John Reid is an English acoustics engineer. For 30 years, until 1999, he was the technical director of Sound Electronics Ltd, a company which specialised in acoustic solutions for churches, cathedrals and public buildings. Currently, in his well-equipped laboratory, he is conducting research into the true nature of sound, its role in the creation of life and the mechanisms by which it heals. He has invented the *CymaScope* a device which manifests sound as 2D slices through the sonic bubble, enabling it to be studied directly through the visual cortex. His interests in the ritualistic use of sound in ancient Egypt led him to become one of only two men who have carried out an acoustic study of the *Great Pyramid,* and the only person to have investigated the King's Chamber sarcophagus, cymatically. Reid is also a poet.

II-5 Herman Ludwig Ferdinand Von Helmholtz (1821-1894) was a German physician and physicist entirely devoted to science. While studying muscle metabolism, he discovered the energy conservation principle. He contributed to the field of sensory physiology as well as medical optics by inventing an instrument to examine the inside of the human eye. With his book *On the sensations of tone as a physiological basis for the theory of music* he enriched the studies of sound and aesthetics. After 1871, the year Helmholtz moved to Berlin to become a professor of physics, his interest in electromagnetism resulted in the *theory of waves* and the first ever demonstration of electromagnetic radiation.

II-6 Pythagoras (Πυθαγορας, 569BC-475BC) was a Greek philosopher who made important contributions to mathematics, astronomy and the theory of music. He was born on the island of Samos, off the coast of Asia Minor, and lived for 22 years in Egypt, 12 years in Babylon and probably spent some time in India prior to settling in Croton (presently Crotone in Southern Italy) where he established a of philosophy modelled on a secret society.

II-7 Leon Batista Alberti (1404-1472) was an Italian writer, architect, philosopher, painter, poet, linguist, cryptographer and musician – a true embodiment of the Renaissance man. In his theoretical works he studied the principles of proportion and harmony, and introduced a humanistic theory of art. In his work *On painting* (1435), he analysed perspective in the architecture of Brunelleschi promoting the language of classical forms and thus breaking from the Gothic past.

II-8   Michael S. Schneider, from his book *A Beginner's Guide to Constructing the Universe – the Mathematical Archetypes of Nature, Art, and Science*. Schneider has a Bachelor's Degree in Mathematics and a M.Ed. in Maths Education. He is an Adjunct Professor at the *California College of the Arts* (San Francisco) where he teaches the numerical language of nature and arts in workshops for teachers, artists, architects, designers and children. The geometry behind some of the statues at the entrance to the *Cathedral of St. John the Divine* in New York City was designed by him. Schneider is also a computer consultant and education writer; www.constructingtheuniverse.com

II-9   Aristotle (Αριστοτέλης, 384BC-322BC), together with Socrates (470BC-399BC) and Plato (Πλάτων, 427BC-347BC), is considered one of the most significant ancient Greek philosophers. Aristotle was Plato's student and a teacher of Alexander the Great. His interests embraced all available knowledge and Aristotle was the encyclopaedia-man of his time. He studied and wrote on topics of science, philosophy, education, literature and poetry. Some of his most important works are *Physics, Metaphysics* (or *Ontology*), *Nicomachean Ethics, Politics, De Anima (On the Soul)* and *Poetics*. Aristotle favoured the empirical way of evaluating data rather than the *a priori* way of intuition or revelation, and thus laid a foundation for the methodology of modern science.

II-10   Suzanne Ward, through mental telepathy, records messages from Matthew, her son from the world of Spirit. Her books *(Matthew Books)* brought about in this way are: *Matthew, tell me about Heaven; Revelations for a new era, Illumination for a new era and Voices of the Universe;* www.matthewbooks.com

II-11   Messages from Angels; www.star-knowledge.net

II-12   Plato (Πλάτων, 427BC-347BC), is considered one of the most significant ancient Greek philosophers. Plato's Academy was built in 428BC, in Athens, on a site continuously inhabited since prehistoric times. The philosophical school gained fame thanks to the Neoplatonists. It existed for more than seven centuries, before Emperor Justinian closed it in the year 347AD.

II-13   Nikola Tesla (1856-1943) was an inventor, electrical and an mechanical engineer, a physicist, and a visionary of profound genius devoted to science and peace. The father of the radio and modern electrical transmission systems, he is often regarded as one of the greatest scientists in the history of technology. Tesla was born to Serbian parents in the Austro-Hungarian Empire (present-day Croatia) where he spent his childhood. The last 56 years of his life Tesla spent in the USA, where he patented 700 inventions. Among them are the alternating current induction motor, Tesla-coils used in radio and television sets, fluorescent lights, wireless communications and the transmission of electrical energy, vertical take-off aircraft, the laser beam, and remote controls and robotics. The use of solar energy and the power of the sea were some of his visions.

II-14   Blaise Pascal (1623-1662) was a French mathematician, religious philosopher and physicist. He wrote on scientific methods, and contributed to the study of fluids by clarifying the concepts of pressure and vacuum. In mathematics he added to the knowledge of projective geometry, probability theory and the construction of a mechanical calculator. Pascal also influenced social sciences and since 1654, after a mystical experience, lived in solitude and wrote about philosophy and theology.

II-15   Paul Gauguin (1848-1903), Paris-born descendant of a South American family, and a leading post-impressionist painter. He was disappointed with European art's lack of symbolism and mystic depth, which he saw in African and Asian artwork, and thus wanted to escape European civilisation. Gauguin found refuge from the artificial and the conventional in the hot tropics, and eventually settled in Polynesia.

II-16   Franz Kafka (1883-1924) was a Czech-born Jewish writer, an icon of the 20th century, noted for his German-language novel *The Trial* and his short stories (the most famous is *Metamorphosis)*. Kafka's work pictures situations of the absurd and the surreal.

II-17   Rudolf Steiner (1861-1925) was an Austrian with a doctorate in philosophy from *The University of Rostock* in Germany, in 1891, with his thesis *Truth and Science*. He was also an architect, educator, social thinker and the founder of anthroposophy. *The Waldorf education system* and *anthroposophical medicine* were his visions, while his inspiration by Göethe led him to defining biodynamic agriculture that in the present time we call organic farming.

II-18   Image inspired by the diagram featured in the message *Universe and Music* from *The Knowledge Book* by Vedia Bülent (Önsü) Çorak, Fascicule 18, pages 277-279

MESSAGES BEHIND SHAPES

III-1   Illustrations by Dr Ibrahim F. Karim: 3.1, 3.2, 3.3, 3.4, 3.5, 3.6, 3.7 and 3.8, reproduced by the kind permission of the author

III-2   Marcel Proust (1871-1922) was a French writer and critic, the author of *Remembrance of things past*. It is a seven-volume work published over 14 years.

III-3   Christina Georgina Rossetti (1830-1894) was an English poet of Italian origin known for religious writing and children's poetry. She was against slavery, war and cruelty to animals

III-4   BioGeometry™ – TM stands for Trade Mark; BG – abbreviation for *BioGeometry*™

III-5   Noel Huntley, PhD, English scientist with a background in physics and doctorates in psychology and parapsychology, also a talented painter and musician, with a keen interest in computers. He has developed the foundation for a spiritual science as well as for the physics of a higher dimensional consciousness. Some of his books are: *ET and ALIENS: Who Are They? And Why Are They Here?; The Scientific Principles of Spiritual Enslavement* and *Attainment of Superior Physical Abilities and the New Science of Body Motion.* His website *Beyond Duality* is a collection of articles on variety of topics, like evolution, the nature of time, ascension, consciousness, holographic civilisation, fractals, types of physics and the theory of one; www.users.globalnet.co.uk/~noelh

III-6   From Dr Ibrahim F. Karim; www.biogeometry.com

III-7   Spasoje Vlajić (BSc in crystallography) has spent more than twenty years researching the area of consciousness, the result of which are numerous books, scientific papers and articles. Some of his books are: *The Formula of Light* (1984), *Healing with Sound and Colours* (1992), *Formula of Consciousness* (1996), *History of the Future* (2000), *Tesla's Millennium's Presents – Formula for Getting One's Wishes True* (2002), *Physics and Technology of Consciousness* (2005). Vlajić lives in Belgrade (Serbia) and teaches information technology.

III-8   Vedia Bülent (Önsü) Çorak, *The Knowledge Book,* Fascicule 16, pages 242-244; Fascicule 34, pages 559-560

III-9   Hafiz (Khwajeh Shams al-Din Muhammad Hafez-e Shirazi) was a 14th century (1310-1337) Persian mystical poet born in Shiraz (present-day Iran). The word *Hafiz* means *Guardian* and in the Muslim world it is used to indicate a person who has memorised the entire *Quran*, such as was the case with the poet Hafiz. He is said to have also memorised the works of Rumi, Nezami, Attar and Sa'di. His poetry, noted for its beauty and wisdom, continues to inspire generations.

III-10   Vedia Bülent (Önsü) Çorak, *The Knowledge Book,* Supplement 6, page 1071, illustration – Milena

III-11   Henry D. Thoreau (1817-1862) was an American pacifist, philosopher, author, transcendentalist, tax resister, and a lifelong activist in fighting to abolish the practice of slavery and the worldwide slave trade. He also wrote on issues of natural history, ecology and the environment.

III-12 For an explanation of the ℞ symbol see *The Knowledge Book,* Vedia Bülent (Önsü) Çorak, Fascicule 23, pages 356-357

III-13 **Richard Amiel McGough**, holds a BSc in Mathematics and Physics from *Washington State University* (1985), and studied Quantum Physics while working on his PhD. He is an expert Web developer, Visual Basic 6.0 developer, ActiveX developer and Microsoft Certified Professional. McGough is the sole author and designer of the BibleWheel.com website. He also published the book: *THE BIBLE WHEEL — A Revelation of the Divine Unity of the Holy Bible*. Both the website and the book are a comprehensive study of *The Bible*, both in Hebrew and Greek, that reveals the numerical base of this sacred book's structural excellence. The website has an astonishing online database with 2335 interlocked identities. It presents a coherent scientific model of *The Bible* as a divinely designed *Wheel of God* attributed with perfect sevenfold symmetry; www.biblewheel.com

III-14 Alphanumerical analysis, Richard Amiel McGough

III-15 Vedia Bülent (Önsü) Çorak, *The Knowledge Book,* Fascicule 14, pages 208-209; Fascicule 16, pages 242-244

III-16 **Galileo Galilei** (1564-1642) was an Italian physicist and philosopher, considered the father of modern astronomy, modern physics and generally the first modern scientist. His contributions to science include, amongst numerous others, the use of mathematics in experimental physics, improvements to the telescope, putting forward the first and second laws of motion and the first principles of relativity. He supported Copernicus by believing in the heliocentric model of the solar system.

III-17 **Djwal Khul**, according to Theosophy (*Theosophical Society* founded in 1875), is an ancient Tibetan Master. He is a spiritual guide of humankind, and a guardian of ancient metaphysical and cosmological knowledge that is at the base of the world's spiritual traditions. As one of the *Mahatmas* (*Mahatma* means *Great Soul* in Sanskrit), he is believed to be involved in overseeing the spiritual growth of individuals and civilisations. His name is mentioned in the works of Alice Bailey where he is described as a Lama, a Master on *The Second Ray of Love-Wisdom*.

III-18 Vedia Bülent (Önsü) Çorak, *The Knowledge Book,* Fascicule 14, pages 205-207; Fascicule 18, pages 277-279

III-19 **Krishna** (the name indicates *Absolute Truth)*, according to various Hindu traditions, is considered a Supreme Person (God) attributed with 108 names some of which are Govinda, Gopala and Hari. Regarding Krishna's historical appearance, it is speculated that he 'died' at the age of 125, in the year 3102BC. His life and philosophy are featured in *The Bhagavad Gita* (literally *the song of the Lord)* which is one of the chapters of the *Mahabharata*. *The Bhagavad Gita* summarises the principles of Hindu philosophy which is revered as a sacred text. Within it, Lord Krishna invites mortals to the infinite Love of the Lord clarifying that loving God means loving the immortal self which, in turn, leads to inner peace and harmony with the entire Cosmos. The liberation messages of the *Bhagavad Gita* are universal and timeless. The full version of the text contains over 100000 verses and around 2.5 million words while, for example, *The Bible* is around 775000 words long. Along with the *Ramayana* and the *Bhagavatam*, the *Mahabharata* comprise three major Sanskrit epics of ancient India that are of immense importance for the Indian spiritual tradition. The *Mahabharata* is the third largest literary epic poem in the world. The Tibetan *Epic of King Gessar,* from the early 11th century, is the longest with more than 20 million words in over one million verses. The second is *Manas,* a poem of the Kyrgyz people. With nearly half a million lines, it is twenty times longer than Homer's *Odyssey*.

III-20 Chinese characters, used in the background design of this chapter, written by Dr Yongzhong Zhang

III-21 Original drawing by Filip Ivović

III-22   From the book Words on a Holistic Man by Nikolai Velimirović (1880-1956), Published by Dragan Srnić, Šabac, Serbia

III-23   Theon of Smyrna (c70-c135) was a Greek philosopher and mathematician influenced by the Pythagoreans. He wrote three books on Plato's philosophy where he gave an explanation of the relationship between astronomy, music and numbers, going into what is today know as *number theory.*

III-24   Vedia Bülent (Önsü) Çorak, *The Knowledge Book,* Supplement 6, pages 1066-1067, illustration – Milena

III-25   Vedia Bülent (Önsü) Çorak, *The Knowledge Book,* Fascicule 43, pages 727-729

III-26   Vedia Bülent (Önsü) Çorak, *The Knowledge Book,* Fascicule 46, pages 778-782; 785-786

III-27   *Beauty Will Save The World* are words from the novel *The Idiot* (1868) by the Russian Fyodor Mikhailovich Dostoevsky (1821-1881) who is considered one of the greatest writers in world literature. He also wrote *Crime and Punishment* (1866) and *The Brothers Karamazov* (1880). Many great 20th century writers were influenced by Dostoevsky, such as Hesse, Camus, Kafka, Hemingway, Proust, Faulkner, Marquez.

III-28   Vedia Bülent (Önsü) Çorak, *The Knowledge Book,* Supplement 6, pages 1068-1069; illustration – Milena

III-29   Vedia Bülent (Önsü) Çorak, *The Knowledge Book,* Supplement 6, pages 1063-1065; The initial crude matter formation (the nucleus of the *Second Universe* formation) is the result of the Atlanta Dimension's Project within the Tranquillity of Silences – Milena

III-30   Gautama Buddha was named Siddhārtha Gautama at birth and lived in ancient India between c563BC-c483BC. He was a spiritual teacher and the historical founder of Buddhism. In a general sense, the word *Buddha* can be used for anyone who becomes enlightened by spiritual cultivation – the purification of the body and mind, the discovery of the true nature of reality, the transcendence of suffering, and the practicing of a moral life through the virtues of the *middle path* and the *noble eightfold path*. *The Dhammapada*, the wisdom of Gautama Buddha consisting of 423 verses in Pali, was recorded some four centuries after Buddha lived.

III-31   *The Schumann-Field* is a magnetic field between the ionosphere and the Earth's surface. Nikola Tesla was the first person to observe it (1905). He called it an energetic matrix for life on Earth – a magnetic field and an information store at the same time. The constant resonance between the Earth's surface and the ionosphere was named after the German physicist Schumann and is considered an Earth wave. The *Schumann resonance* can fluctuate between 7.8Hz and 45Hz, but most often moves between 9Hz and 12Hz which corresponds to the *alpha* range of human brain activity in a relaxed but awake state.

III-32   From the theatre play: *Tesla or accommodation of an Angel*, by Stevan Pešić, National Theatre Belgrade Publication.

III-33   Karen Davies designs and makes items out of glass. She works with the copper-foiling methods devised by Tiffany, and for stained glass windows she employs traditional leading, glass painting and firing techniques. An award winning artist, Davies works to commission in both commercial and domestic settings and supplies galleries nationwide with her work; www. karendaviesstainedglass.co.uk

Front cover: Detail of the *Dimension of the All-Truthful*
Graphic design of the book: zodrag@gmail.com

BIBLIOGRAPHY

ANTI-GRAVITY & THE WORLD GRID, edited by David Hatcher Childress; Adventures Unlimited Press
- THE ANCIENT SECRETS OF THE FLOWER OF LIFE, Volume 1 & 2 by Drunvalo Melchizedek; Sedona Color Graphics
- A BEGINNER'S GUIDE TO CONSTRUCTING THE UNIVERSE – The mathematical archetypes of Nature, Art, and Science a voyage from 1 to 10 by Michael S. Schneider; Harper Perennial, a division of Harper Collins Publishers
- CELTIC SPIRALS – handbook by Sheila Sturrock; Guild of Master Craftsman Publication Ltd
- FENG SHUI – The Traditional Oriental Way to Enhance Your Life by Stephen Skinner; Siena book, an imprint of Parragon
- THE FRACTAL GEOMETRY OF NATURE by Benoit B. Mandelbrot; W. H. Freeman and Company, New York
- THE GEOMETRY OF ART AND LIFE by Matila Ghyka; Dover Publications, inc. New York
- HIDDEN NATURE – The Startling Insights of Viktor Schauberger by Alick Bartholomew; Floris Books
- THE IMPLOSIONS' GRAND ATTRACTOR – Sacred Geometry & Coherent Emotion; assembled, Edited & Distributed from Daniel Winter's writing by Implosion Group
- ISLAMIC PATTERNS – An Analytical and Cosmological Approach by Keith Critchlow; Thames and Hudson, London
- JUST SIX NUMBERS – The Deep Forces that Shape the Universe by Martin Rees; Weidenfeld & Nicolson – London
- THE KNOWLEDGE BOOK – Messages received and transformed into writing by Vedia Bülent (Önsü) Çorak; World Brotherhood Union Mevlana Supreme Foundation, Istanbul
- L' ASTROLOGIE SACRE – Miroir de la Grande Tradition, Frederic Lionel; Editions du Rocher, Monaco
- LET THE NUMBERS GUIDE YOU – The Spiritual Science of Numerology by Shiv Charan Singh; O Books, Winchester, UK; New York, USA
- MAGIC SYMBOLS by Frederick Goodman; Brian Trodd Publishing House Limited
- THE MASTER MASONS OF CHARTRES by John James; West Grinstead Publishing
- NATURE'S NUMBERS – Discovering Order And Pattern In The Universe by Ian Stewart; Weidenfeld & Nicolson – London
- NUMEROLOGY with Tantra, Ayurveda, and Astrology – A Key to Human Behaviour by Harish Johari; Destiny Books, Rochester, Vermont
- ORDER IN SPACE – A Design Source Book by Keith Critchlow; Thames and Hudson, London
- PATTERN AND DESIGN WITH DYNAMIC SYMMETRY – How to Create Art Deco Geometrical Design by Edward B. Edwards; Dover Publications, inc, New York
- RANDOMNESS by Deborah J. Bennett; Harvard University Press, Cambridge, Massachusetts, London England
- SACRED GEOMETRY by Miranda Lundy; Wooden Books Ltd
- SACRED GEOMETRY – Philosophy and practice by Robert Lawlor; Thames and Hudson
- SECRETS OF ANCIENT AND SACRED PLACES – The world's Mysterious Heritage by Paul Devereux; Brockhampton Press, London
- SUNLIGHT ON WATER – A Manual for Soul-full Living – The One With No Names through Flo Aeveia Magdalena
- SYMMETRY IN CHAOS – A Search for Pattern in mathematics, Art and Nature by Michael Field and Martin Golubitsky; Oxford University Press
- THE JOY OF PI by David Plather; Bath Press Colourbooks, Glasgow
- THE SECRET SCIENCE OF ECSTASY AND IMMORTALITY – IMPLOSION by Daniel Winter
- THE TRUE POWER OF WATER – Healing And Discovering Ourselves by Masaru Emoto; Beyond Words Publishing, Inc., Hillsboro, Oregon
- YANTRA – The Tantric Symbol of Cosmic Unity by Madhu Khanna; Thames and Hudson

Published by
M PUBLISHING
www.memento13.com

A catalogue record for this book is available from
the British Library

ISBN
978-1-909323-15-5